THE HOTTON REPORT

THE HOTTON REPORT

Robert K. McDonald

Gil —
My deepest thanks
for your generous
contributions to this
2nd edition
Aim straight and
stay low!
Bob
10/31/12

FINBAR PRESS

SECOND EDITION

Library of Congress Control Number: 2006938255

ISBN: 0-9665753-8-5

Published by Finbar Press
Post Office Box 987
Hayesville, NC 28904
http://www.finbarpress.com

Printed in the United States of America

10 9 8 7 6 5 4 3 2

Cover Photo: Lt. Colonel Sam Hogan
Back Cover Photo: Lieutenant Jack Warden
            and members of his Task Force

for my father

The art of war is simple enough.
Find out where your enemy is.
Get at him as soon as you can.
Strike at him as hard as you can and as often as you can.
And keep moving on.

— Ulysses S. Grant
General-in-Chief of the Union Armies (1864-1865)

No soldier outlives a thousand chances.
But every soldier believes in Chance and trusts his luck.

— Erich Maria Remarque
All Quiet on the Western Front

FOREWORD

SEVERAL YEARS AGO I GOT A CALL FROM A YOUNG MAN CONcerning a little known battle that occurred in the closing days of 1944. He had heard that my co-author, Steven L. Ossad, and I were about to publish a biography on the life and death of Major General Maurice Rose, the legendary commander of the 3rd Armored Division. His father had served under Rose and had participated in the battle. He wanted to discuss certain inconsistencies he had identified in the various battle accounts he had read. My curiosity piqued, I asked what he planned to do with the information he was gathering. He replied, "I think there's a story here, and I'd like to take a stab at getting it down."

The caller was Bob McDonald and he was talking about the Belgian crossroads village of Hotton, which for several days was at the epicenter of the Second World War. I also had come across differing accounts of the Hotton battle over the years. I advised him the story appeared to have many legs that could lead anywhere or nowhere, especially as it occurred in the fluid first days of what would become known as the Battle of the Bulge. But I couldn't have agreed more that it was a story worth telling, typical as it was of many hard-fought actions by isolated and outnumbered American forces during that bitterly cold Christmas season.

In December 1944, the Allied Expeditionary Forces under General Dwight D. Eisenhower were caught sleeping by Hitler's surprise offensive through the Ardennes region of Belgium and Luxembourg. Tens of thousands of troops scrambled to plug the gaping holes in the American lines, shocked by the strength of the assault. Among them was General Rose, the mustang officer who had risen from the rank of Private to command the elite 3rd Armored Division, and who suddenly found himself in his toughest fight without the firepower of two of his three combat commands. Complicating matters, terrible weather had grounded the Allied planes that dominated the skies of Europe. Fighting "blind" without reconnaissance and air cover was a new challenge for Rose. His reputation for aggressiveness had been established while spearheading the Army's VII Corps across France and Belgium into Germany. Now the tables were turned. Stripped of the bulk of his forces, he was ordered to defend an extended line through unfamiliar terrain while answering to the demands of his equally aggressive superior, General Mathew Ridgway. Rose in turn leaned hard on the commanding officer of his remaining combat command, Colonel Robert Howze, who directed a mixed bag of incredibly brave men from several units.

Until now, the battle for Hotton ranked in the top tier of worthy but untold stories of World War II. McDonald has sifted through the facts to give us the brutal picture of those determined troops who held this vital crossroads "at all cost." His characterization of the soldiers who fought there is a moving tribute to their courage.

Don R. Marsh
Co-author, *Major General Maurice Rose:*
World War II's Greatest Forgotten Commander

The Verdin House after the battle.

Prologue

I WAS TWELVE WHEN HE RETIRED FROM THE ARMY TO BEGIN A second career as a county administrator. Then forty-five, he had spent half his life as a soldier, including five years of intensive training and combat during World War II. Like many sons and daughters born to veterans of that epic struggle, I knew little of what he had actually done. He never spoke of the *in extremis* conditions he had endured: the endless exhaustion, the filth, the chronic constipation, and especially the harsh reality of combat. I vaguely assumed the reason nothing was said was out of consideration for my mother, whose first husband had been killed in the war. Still, I sensed that he had done something important judging from the stacked-up rows of bright-colored ribbons that adorned his uniform. And of course I had seen the scars, pock-mark-like holes on his torso and back, some the size of dimes, the gash on his nose, and, as he began to lose his hair, the thin jagged line where his scalp had been sewn back into place. He explained these telltale markings like they were lint on a jacket: "Oh, just some scratches I picked up in the war." That's the most I ever got from him, and once a teenager I frankly lost interest.

I was twenty-two the last time I saw him. I had come home on a school break and was packing to head back when he asked me to join him in his bedroom. My parents had traded their king bed for twins, and we sat down across from each other. He lit a cigarette, opened the drawer of the table between us, and handed me a sheet of paper. On it, neatly typed, was a list of bank accounts, insurance policies, and a phone number for the Veterans Administration. "What's this?" I asked. "Son, just listen." He proceeded to tell me what to do upon his death, silencing my protests with a wave of his hand. Then, leading me to his closet, he unzipped a black garment bag revealing the dress-blue uniform I had last seen as a boy. "I want to be buried in this," he said, "and I want to be buried at Arlington. Call that number. They'll handle the arrangements."

Six weeks later he was struck down by a heart attack while golfing. Pursuant to the idiot-proof instructions with which he had entrusted me, he was buried at Arlington National Cemetery with full military honors befitting a Lieutenant Colonel and a combat veteran. After the funeral, huddled over pitchers of green beer, his children talked about the father we had lost.

Clarence Michael McDonald — he went by Mike — was born in Harlem just steps from Morningside Park, the son of a city bus driver with an eighth grade education and a newly arrived redhead from County Cork, Ireland. When he was three, the family moved to Long Beach, Long Island, where his father joined the fire department while moonlighting as a handy man and real estate agent renting summer houses near the Boardwalk. It was an idyllic place to grow up, and growing up, my father's life revolved around three interests: sports, girls and the Army. There was nothing unusual in the first two — after all, New York had a rich history of big league teams, and most boys were intrigued by girls. But there also was nothing in his family tree to steer him toward the military. Where or from whom he got the idea is unclear. Certainly he was aware from his paper route days and movie newsreels of the growing belligerence by

Germany and Japan; maybe it represented sure employment to a depression-era kid with an itch to see the world. In any case, in 1940, he became the first in the family to don a uniform when he joined the National Guard of New York as a Private. Two years later, he was selected for Officer Candidates School, promoted to Second Lieutenant, and assigned to a unit then training in the California desert for deployment to North Africa.

That was the extent of what we knew of his early life when, in late 2000, I came across a letter he had written to me shortly before his death. At first glance, the letter appeared typical of his weekly *epistles* as he liked to call them, a breezy update on all that was happening at home followed by a posting of everyone's plans. It went on to relate his excitement about an upcoming trip to New York City to watch me play football against Columbia, whose hapless Lions were then winless through two seasons and seemed poised to extend their streak indefinitely. Toward the end his tone turned somber as he referred to a conversation we evidently had had in which I inquired about his war experience. "I still haven't had time to let you live part of my life in each letter. However, attached is a copy of a letter I wrote 30 years ago to Monsignor Cass (now deceased) our Parish priest .... This is really nostalgic, Bob — I'm not sure we can continue this game."

The enclosed letter, dated October 17, 1944, had been reprinted in a church bulletin under the caption "From One of My First Two Altar Boys." It read in part:

> We are off the restricted list these days, so it's safe to say we were the unit that went through Belgium in 11 days and then cracked the famed Siegfried line in another day. It was tough but worth it as

units behind us had fairly easy sailing. Perhaps next time it will be reversed, and we may be fortunate to hit the easy sector.

In France things were different . . . . At St. Lo we considered 200 yards a good day's work. The hardest battle of all was at Mortain where we caught the brunt of the German 7th Army counter-attack. I lost so many friends there that I will never forget that place.

My personal experiences have been many but God has been good to me and seen fit to spare me. Guess there were times when I didn't believe I would live but somehow He always seemed at my side and kept pushing the shells away from me. I believe a thousand miracles a day take place in war, Father, because God deems it better for some to live just a little longer.

Our chaplain is really a prince. He's from Indiana and his name is Father Kraka. He holds the Purple Heart medal now which proves what sort of a man he really is to the boys.

At the bottom of the page, stamped in italics, were the words *Let Nothing Affright Thee.*

Remarkably, I had only a dim recollection of the Cass letter. Reading it again, I found myself transfixed by my father's words — and troubled that I had not followed through on a rare, and as it turned out, fleeting invitation to explore his past. That evening I telephoned my uncle to tell him what I had found.

"It sounds like Dad saw quite a bit of combat," I said.

"Oh hell yes," he replied, himself a Marine veteran of the fighting in the Pacific. "He ran a reconnaissance platoon with the 3rd Armored Division. In fact, he got into a scrape later on that landed him in all the New York papers."

"Where was that?"

"Somewhere in Belgium. They were defending a bridge as I recall."

If you've ever taken a hard whack to the head, then you can appreciate the dizzy, where-am-I feeling that ensued following this call. Questions began to hound me. Why was I just learning of this now? Why was I surprised my father may have distinguished himself in combat? And why had he characterized my curiosity concerning his past as a *game?* Over the next weeks hardly a day passed that I didn't catch myself daydreaming about the man I had known in my youth. Images and snippets of conversation trickled back. I recalled, for instance, his queer, almost obsessive, habit of panning the sky for planes. "That's a C-47," he might have said, pointing up at some glimmering dot in the distance. "You can tell by the wing angle and fin." Or his admonition while teaching me to drive to "maintain your march distance," which I somehow understood to mean "don't tailgate." But the remark that kept coming back was something he said to my brother when he left for Vietnam. "Remember Michael, stay low." *Stay low.* What I thought of this at the time, if anything, is lost to me.

The problem was that I could not reconcile the civilian I remembered best with the young soldier I had recently encountered. The man I knew had morphed into a 40-inch waist, wore striped shirts with plaid trousers, and seemed incapable of matching his socks. The only photograph I had of him in uniform was from my parents' wedding in 1946, which, upon reexamination, showed a distinctly confident man. But there were no pictures of him in combat gear, no war souvenirs, no journals — in short, nothing to assist me in visualizing him during this period. My gut told me I had to fill the gap between the gregarious but selectively reticent civil servant I had observed as a boy, and the seasoned soldier who suddenly had emerged from the faded xerox of an old letter.

I found the newspaper stories my uncle had mentioned, which identified that *somewhere in Belgium* as a place called Hotton, a pinprick of a village some fifty miles south of Liège. The *scrape* to which he had referred began on the morning of December 21, 1944, five days after the launch of Hitler's audacious counter-offensive later known as the Battle of the Bulge. Thin on specifics, the stories reported a David-against-Goliath battle between a small, isolated American force comprised of rear-guard troops, and elements of a German *Panzer* division intent on capturing Hotton's logistically important bridge. (The articles did not explain why the bridge was important.) In one account, published in the *New York Sun*, my father was credited with destroying three German tanks; in another, from the *Nassau Daily Review-Star*, he reportedly "knocked out six tanks, two half tracks and one truck, and it is estimated that he killed or wounded nearly one hundred enemy soldiers. Hotten [*sic*], a little crossroads village, but an important military objective, was saved by Lieutenant McDonald." The emotions I experienced while reading these stories were numbing.

But it was an article in the Army weekly *Yank* titled "The Cooks and the Clerks" that provided the most detailed and colorful account of the action. Drawn from contemporaneous interviews with two-dozen soldiers from the 3rd Armored Division, it described a three-day battle involving a "hundred-odd" cooks, clerks, engineers, radio operators and mechanics — armed only with rifles, a few machine guns and bazookas, and one mortar squad directed by my father — against "a full battalion of [German] infantry plus 14 tanks and supporting artillery." By my arithmetic, this meant the Americans had been outnumbered about ten-to-one, excluding the enemy's formidable weaponry. Inspiring as it was, the article did not explain *how* this ragtag group of lightly-armed GIs "not rated as combat soldiers" had prevailed in the face of such staggering odds, and at the cost of "very light" casualties.

Indeed, the further I delved into the events at Hotton the more unclear it became what had happened. Units unmentioned in any of the early accounts — most notably the 51st Engineer Combat Battalion and the 517th Parachute Regimental Combat Team — emerged to claim credit for the victory with hardly a nod to the beleaguered troops of the 3rd Armored. In one especially perplexing first-hand account, the battle did not even begin until the afternoon of December 24th — *after* the fighting in the village had supposedly ended — and involved, on the American side, a single depleted platoon of eighteen men supported by four tanks. Significantly, the author of the piece insisted there were no other Americans in the village except for a few engineers hiding in a cellar. Not only was I unsure which version of history to trust, I questioned whether people were even talking about the same battle.

Fortunately, the Army in World War II kept meticulous records of its activities. Unit histories, daily logs, after-action reports, interviews with ground commanders, and maps formatted to the military system of grid blocks and six-digit coordinates, made it possible to reconstruct a reasonably precise timeline of the events in Hotton, and to identify which units were there. Yet indispensable as these resources were, they provided little information about the soldiers doing the fighting, and little flavor of the conditions on the ground. It was like seeing the earth from the moon.

I tracked down a few of them mentioned by name in the various battle accounts, including one veteran who was living at the same address he had given on enlistment in 1942. Through them, I gradually gained access to a network of forgotten soldiers who had not only been there, but were eager to discuss what most considered the signal event of their lives.

This is their story, and in a sense my own.

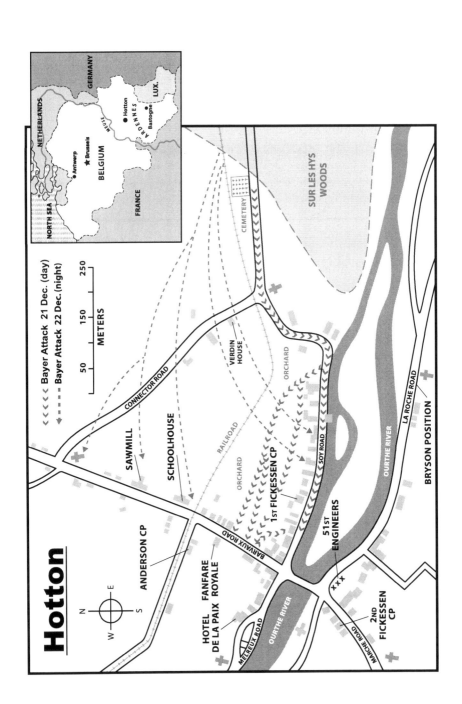

Hotton

N
W — E
S

≪≪≪ Bayer Attack 21 Dec. (day)
----- Bayer Attack 22 Dec. (night)

METERS
50   150   250

CONNECTOR ROAD

SAWMILL

SCHOOLHOUSE

VERDIN
HOUSE

RAILROAD

ORCHARD

ORCHARD

CEMETERY

SUR LES HYS
WOODS

ANDERSON CP

1ST FICKESSEN CP

SOY ROAD

51ST
ENGINEERS

BARVAUX ROAD

HOTEL
FANFARE
DE LA PAIX ROYALE

MELREUX ROAD

OURTHE RIVER

2ND
FICKESSEN
CP

MARCHE ROAD

OURTHE RIVER

LA ROCHE ROAD

BRYSON POSITION

NORTH SEA

NETHERLANDS

GERMANY

BELGIUM
★ Brussels
● Antwerp

FRANCE

MEUSE

● Hotton

ARDENNES

● Bastogne

LUX.

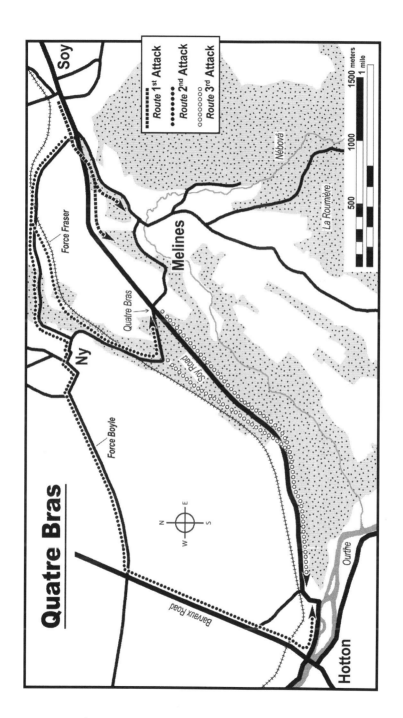

Quatre Bras

Soy

Ny

Force Fraser

Force Boyle

Quatre Bras

Soy Road

Barvaux Road

Melines

Nébová

La Roumière

Ourthe

Hotton

Route 1st Attack
Route 2nd Attack
Route 3rd Attack

500   1000   1500 meters
                1 mile

N
E
S
W

21

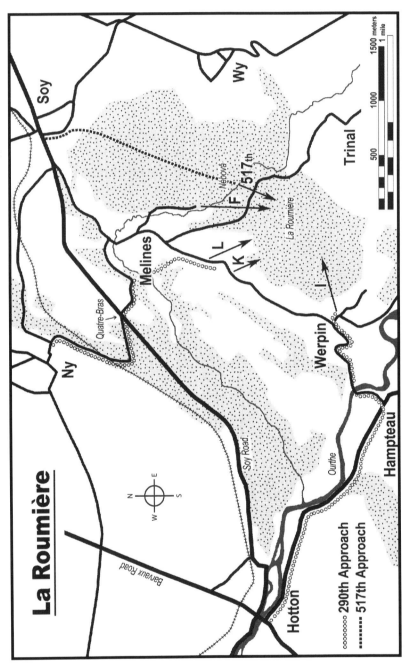

La Roumière

22

Soy

Wy

Trinal

Néboya

F 517th

La Roumière

Melines

L

K

Quatre-Bras

I

Ny

Werpin

Soy Road

Ourthe

Hampteau

Barvaux Road

Hotton

N
W E
S

ooooooo 290th Approach
---------- 517th Approach

1500 meters
1 mile
1000
500

01

THE VILLAGE OF HOTTON STRADDLES THE OURTHE River on the southwestern slope of the Belgian Ardennes, twelve miles downstream from the old city of LaRoche and thirty-three miles from the German frontier. Between LaRoche and Hotton, the north-flowing Ourthe carves a meandering path through the high craggy hills of the Ardennes forest rendering it, until recent years, largely uncrossable except by footbridge. At Hotton, the green canyon cliffs of rock and trees, mostly fir, pine and oak, abruptly give way to a wide rolling plain and a network of roads leading west to the Belgian coast and south into France.

In 1944, the village had changed relatively little since its debut on a crude 12th century map. Most of its thousand-odd souls still reaped a living from the land in one fashion or another, bought their bread at the same *boulangerie* passed down through generations, and huddled in quaint solid homes along the river, their collective identity tied inextricably to the bridge that connected them. Yet for all its rustic charm and lush backdrop of brooding hills, Hotton was known principally for its access to other places.

Its longest-standing bridge, built in 1770 during the reign of Austrian monarch Maria-Thérèse and nostalgically depicted in the village coat-of-arms, was a muscular structure of wide arches and limestone cut from a nearby quarry. Condemned in 1895, it was replaced with an iron bridge in a grudging bow to the industrial revolution that had produced the Eiffel Tower six years earlier. The locals never warmed to its busy architecture, deriding it as a masterpiece of inelegance until, in 1940, it was blown up by the Belgian Army in an attempt to slow the thundering advance of Hitler's *Wehrmacht* into France. German engineers promptly hauled off the twisted steel and constructed a timber bridge in its place, only to blow it themselves in September 1944 in an attempt to slow the American advance to the Motherland. Their bridge-building skills, however, were such that it required two attempts to fully bring it down, after which, as a parting gesture, German guns took aim at most of the buildings on the south bank, including Hotton's only church (Catholic), which lost its steeple to a high-explosive tank round. Within days, American combat engineers had put up their own two-way timber bridge sturdy enough to support anything on wheels or tracks up to 70-tons, reuniting the village once again and establishing a secure supply route to the German front.

Three roads converged at the bridge. The main highway entered the village from the northern town of Barvaux and proceeded southwest across the bridge to the city of Marche. A second road on the north bank dropped down from the densely wooded hills to the east and nearby village of Soy, past a square stone-walled cemetery where it curved sharply toward the river and an ancient grain mill, then continued west beyond the bridge to the village of Melreux. The third road, on the south bank, hugged the rock cliffs along the Ourthe from Hotton to La Roche. In World War II, the Americans, like the Germans before them, never bothered to learn the actual names of these roads. Rather, they identified them simply by where they led; thus, the main highway became "Barvaux Road" on the north bank and "Marche Road" on the south; the river road was "Soy Road" to the east of the bridge and "Melreux Road" to the west; and the road to LaRoche was just that, "LaRoche Road." Punctuating each of the main roads where they exited the village was a tiny squat chapel, five of them in all, put there for travelers so that they might pray for protection en route to wherever it was they were going.

In addition to these main arteries there were two smaller roads on the north bank: one followed a single-track rail line from Melreux that came to a T at the schoolhouse on Barvaux Road three hundred yards from the bridge, from which point the rail line continued east on an elevated embankment toward Soy Road; the other, perpetually muddy, connected Barvaux Road and Soy Road where they entered the village and ran parallel to the encroaching hills. On the south bank, a thin strip of asphalt climbed from Marche Road to a high bluff from which the village could be viewed in panorama.

Hotton's finest homes faced the river on Soy Road – both of the village's two doctors lived there – behind which were well-tended gardens and a broad orchard dotted with fruit trees that extended north to the railroad embankment. A scattering of smaller homes lined Barvaux Road, along with the new *Fanfare Royale* movie theatre, the schoolhouse and a lumber mill. The schoolhouse was by far the most prominent building in the village. Built in 1868 of brick and stone and thoroughly imposing for its day, the two-story Georgian-style building was wrapped with tall windows that offered unobstructed views of the surrounding countryside, especially east to the green hills above the cemetery and the several farmhouses situated along the connector road.

In December 1944, with their new bridge and shot-up church undergoing repairs, *les Hottonnais* were feeling cautiously optimistic about the future. The Germans, or *les Boches* as they referred to them, had been gone three months, replaced by the seemingly relaxed troops of the 51st Engineer Combat Battalion which had taken over some thirty lumber mills in the area churning out construction timber for the American First Army. Hopeful the war was behind them, villagers busied themselves in preparation for Christmas. Floors were scrubbed, candles appeared in windows, cupboards stocked with special foods. The sound of music wafted through the close-knit community as choirs rehearsed their repertoire of carols and children wished for snow, their bright faces flushed with holiday distractions. Their worst fear, to the extent they harbored one, was that their children's wishes would be answered too well, dumping heavy snows in the Ardennes causing the Ourthe to overflow its banks come spring. This happened every twenty years or so, and they were due. But spring was a long way off, and perhaps in a world of competing prayers they would be blessed with a mild winter.

The Hotton Bridge, December 1944.

The Hotton Church on the south bank of the Ourthe in September 1944, following the German retreat.

02

THE 51ST ENGINEER COMBAT BATTALION HAD BEEN HEAD-quartered in Marche since October, its 599 enlisted men and 34 officers visible in the surrounding villages, managing the sawmills and enjoying life in the rear: hot meals, regular hours, the occasional movie. Convoys ferrying supplies and troop replacements rolled through Marche and Hotton heading north and east to the front, places like Aachen and Stolberg and Monschau inside Germany where the fighting had stalled. In three months not a single engineer had fired a weapon at the enemy and none had been fired upon. Like the majority of Americans in Europe, they believed the war was nearly over, or would be by spring when the Allies would close on Berlin.

On December 14th, Lieutenant Colonel Harvey Fraser arrived to take command of the 51st. The 28 year-old West Pointer had lobbied long and hard for a combat assignment. Energetic and extremely bright, Fraser had graduated 10th in his class of 456 cadets, an achievement that had earned him a peach assignment to the lush island outpost at Schofield Barracks in Hawaii. On the morning of December 7, 1941, Fraser was packed to return to the States when Japanese fighter-bombers struck the blow that catapulted America into the Second World War. His transfer postponed, Fraser stayed another nine months repairing roads and airstrips pulverized in the surprise attack, all the while pleading for assignment deeper in the Pacific nearer to the action. Instead he was sent to Camp Drum, a frigid outpost on the New York-Canadian border, where he honed his skills erecting and dismantling bridges, laying and removing mines, setting explosives, clearing obstacles, and otherwise mastering the art of combat engineering. In July of 1944, following the Allied invasion of France, he found himself in Brittany doing yet more roadwork. Again he requested a combat assignment, which now, finally, had been approved.

Initially he must have wondered if he was the victim of a joke. Not only was Marche far from any fighting, none of the troops from the 51st had seen combat since arriving in Europe. Fraser's review of the unit's daily log for December proved quick reading. Except for some flying bomb activity and two court-martials, nothing of note had happened. Output at the sawmills averaged 98,000 linear board feet daily, about 18 miles-worth laid end-to-end; it had rained practically every day; and there was a shortage of overshoes — sizes 10, 11 and 12 — along with certain "badly needed blank forms." He spent the first two days touring sawmills, getting to know the men and, according to the daily log, "outlining his policies and desires in a very coherent manner." Fraser's central message in these introductory pep talks was a simple one, namely, that they were soldiers first, lumbermen second, and must be prepared to fight.

It was a timely reminder. At 5:30 on the afternoon of December 17th — 1730 hours on a military clock — the 51st was alerted to "ground activity" in the area. Fraser immediately called a staff meeting to plan a defense against attack, and ordered that his half-track — a hybrid vehicle with wheels up front and tank-like treads aft — be readied to serve as his mobile command post. At 1800 he sent one of his three companies to the village of Trois Ponts, an important road center on the Ambleve River to the northeast, with orders to set roadblocks and prepare two bridges for demolition. By 0500 on the 18th, Fraser's remaining forces, numbering approximately 400 men, had loaded all weapons and were awaiting orders.

The city of Marche, meanwhile, looked like Grand Central Station at rush hour. Streets were congested with civilians evacuating to the west, interspersed with increasing numbers of Americans fleeing to the rear, many of them without rifles, their clothes ripped and morale shattered, all asking the same questions: "Where is my unit? How far have the Germans broken through?" Fraser had witnessed such confusion following the bombing of Pearl Harbor. He knew it was essential to keep the roads clear so that he could deploy his remaining forces, and to make room for reinforcements if they came. To do this he established a clearing station to record the names of these dispirited "birds of passage" to aid in returning them to their units when things settled down, and with help from the local *gendarmerie*, formed check points to ensure that the civilians trudging west, bags in hand, were in fact civilians. Like everyone else, he had heard rumors of German paratroopers dropped behind American lines to sow confusion.

By that afternoon, Fraser's men in Trois Ponts had blown two bridges across the Ambleve River; four of his men were killed defending the third bridge by a single round from an 88-mm cannon. At 1900, Fraser was designated Defense Commander of the Ourthe River area from Durby to LaRoche, including Hotton. Over the next 24 hours, the 51st would prepare six bridges for demolition, establish concentrated firing positions at ten key road junctions, and lay down three minefields. In Hotton, two fire teams were set up on the south bank of the bridge, each comprised of a 40-mm *Bofors* gun, a .50 caliber machine gun, and a bazooka. A small fire team had also been set up on the south side of the footbridge in Hampteau, a mile and a half upriver from Hotton. Except for Fraser's skeleton staff and a few military police, every last man and weapon were now deployed at choke points along the Ourthe. For the moment there was nothing else for Fraser — already tagged with the moniker "Hurry Up Harvey" — to do but wait.

* * *

ON THE MORNING OF DECEMBER 19TH, CHAPLAIN JOHN Kraka was in Stolberg pecking at a captured German typewriter while listening to the steady cough of vehicles moving west. His desk on the ground floor of the abandoned *Kerpen Kabel und Gummiwerk* factory was illuminated by a single light bulb suspended from a steel girder overhead, the cord fed through a broken window to his jeep idling outside. He was writing a letter to the parents of a soldier killed in France the previous August, a young lieutenant whose enthusiasm for song was exceeded only by a willingness to throw himself in harm's way. Kraka had admired him enormously, and the letter — his *ninety-ninth* condolence note in just over a month — took longer than he would have liked given the backlog of families still to be solaced. The machine's unfamiliar placement of characters and peculiar umlauts and sharp S did not help matters; but what weighed him down was the image of his friend laid out on an oxcart, his corpse covered with flowers placed there by villagers to mask the massive hole in his chest. The letter did not mention this. Rather, Kraka spoke of their son's cheerfulness and courage, and the righteousness of the cause which had summoned him home, and concluded with a prayer that they might see in every sorrow the guiding finger of God.

His painful chore completed, the 37 year-old priest twisted sideways in his chair to discharge a slurry of tobacco juice into a bucket, feeling the butt of a pistol beneath his field jacket as he did so. That he was prohibited under military regulations from wielding a firearm carried little weight with Kraka, especially now as the Division prepared to retreat for the first time since coming ashore at Omaha Beach six months earlier.

Kraka had quit school in eighth grade to join his father in an Indiana coalmine. For the next six years he toiled underground – "digging and loading" as he later described it – where he became hardened by the backbreaking work and the turn-no-cheek ethos of his environment. When his father was crippled in a mine explosion, he set out for Detroit and a metal stamping job at a Chevrolet plant. Finding the conditions there only marginally better than what he left behind, the young Kraka sought the counsel of his hometown priest who arranged a scholarship for him at a Catholic boys' school in Kentucky. Then twenty-one he never looked back, grinding his way through high school, college, and a Benedictine seminary in seven years.

The men of the 36th Armored Infantry Regiment initially weren't sure what to make of the hard-drinking priest with the boxer's face and ever-present plug of Mail Pouch tobacco. They soon learned, however, not to snicker during his lectures on such subjects as "Sexual Morality" and "Reverence of God's Name While on Bivouac," much less argue his umpiring calls in regimental baseball games. But what won their hearts was his insistence on being near them in combat.

At 1240 hours, the remaining troops of the 3rd Armored Division were put on three-hour alert to move out. Kraka and his clerk had already packed their bedrolls and few belongings, the quirky typewriter, and Mass kit containing the priest's vestments, altar cloth and candles, sacred vessels, and supplies of hosts and wine into the jeep and trailer outside. Kraka went to the doorway to observe the commotion. Up the street the Prym House hummed with activity as staff officers and messengers came and went. The Division's 45 year-old commander, Major General Maurice Rose, had personally selected the four-story mansion to be his Advance Command Post, converting its magnificent dining room into a mess hall to provide hot meals for his men when they were not on patrol or out-posted along the perimeter of the American-held sector of town. It was overcast and cold, the temperature in the low-thirties. Kraka watched drivers fuel their vehicles from five-gallon cans and perform basic maintenance while awaiting specific march orders. He saw Charlie Kapes and Phil Zulli standing in the street. Both were regulars to his rectory at the cable and rubberworks factory, with whom he had often shared scotch while talking baseball.

As he approached them, Kraka could not decide which of the two looked worse. Kapes, the Division's Provost Marshall, had been up two days directing traffic and relocating prisoners to Liège. Zulli fidgeted in pain, fresh off the operating table where doctors had snipped a particularly awful case of hemorrhoids the day before. Kraka chided him for being on his feet. The popular Zulli stoically replied that a day without piles was better than Christmas.

"Where to?" said Kraka.

"Belgium," said Kapes. "About sixty miles southwest of here. Command is still hammering out the details."

The three of them lingered for a few moments speculating on the various rumors circulating through camp. Kapes turned to go.

"Padre," he said, glancing at Zulli. "See if you can talk this Wop into some bed rest. It hurts just looking at him."

* * *

WHAT WAS LEFT OF MAURICE ROSE'S CELEBRATED 3RD Armored Division began its pullout from Germany at 1640 hours, a shade after sunset, the general himself riding shotgun in an open jeep at the tip of the column.

Rose was revered by his men and all were familiar with his story: a private at seventeen, his bravery and wounding in World War I, his ascendance – without ever attending college – to Chief of Staff under General George Patton in North Africa. They saw a leader of almost mystic self-confidence who inspired the same in them, and a fearless soldier who could inevitably be found wherever the action was hottest. It didn't hurt that at six-feet-two and 185 pounds, the always composed and impeccably dressed Rose embodied what they thought a general should look like. Yet despite this universal respect, there were those who also saw an ambitious warrior perhaps too willing to spill their blood along with his own to achieve an objective.

The handsome Rose was in a dark mood. His two main Combat Commands representing the bulk of his tankers, infantry and heavy weapons had been attached to other units, leaving him with only Combat Command Reserve, or CCR, to carry out his as yet undefined mission. Senior Allied commanders were still wrapping their minds around the stunning German attack launched three days earlier, which already had claimed thousands of American casualties and captured, astronomical numbers that were certain to mount. The dearth of solid intelligence was exasperating. Rotten weather had grounded their planes so no one knew exactly where the enemy was, only that they were advancing en masse into the dense forests of the Ardennes. Hitler was intimately familiar with the Ardennes as his *Werhmacht* had crossed this formidable terrain to invade France in 1940. Now, entire divisions had been overrun while others, such as Rose's 3rd Armored, were falling back to plug the breach in the American lines.

Of the roughly 4,500 men riding in the column behind him, buttoned up as best they could in the freezing drizzle and thickening fog, less than a third were battle-tested soldiers. The rest were rear-guard troops — supply personnel, mechanics, engineers, wiremen, clerks and cooks — charged with keeping his tankers and infantry supplied with ammunition and fuel, water and food, repairing vehicles, clearing obstacles, and maintaining communication between and among the various units. Offsetting Rose's concerns was a profound confidence in the fighting men he did have, and in the abilities of his unit commanders to squeeze the most from the resources available to them.

As Rose sped off with the benefit of headlights to illuminate the road ahead, the rest of the column — some 700 vehicles stretching more than eight miles — slogged along in deteriorating weather under blackout, their taillights taped into narrow cat-eyes. At Aachen the column turned south into the rugged terrain of the Belgian Ardennes. Vehicles quickly piled up in the black fog or left the ice-slick roads altogether, crashing into trees or mired in mud so thick they were passed by until maintenance could winch them back onto the road. It was 2200 before CCR at the tail of the column reached Verviers, having covered just twenty miles in four hours. If nerves weren't frayed enough, low-flying bombs chugged overhead like old tractors followed by a sickening lull as their engines stalled and the thousand-pound charges fell to earth. An hour after he shoved off, one of these "buzz" bombs landed a hundred yards from Rose's speeding jeep. The resulting concussion sent his aide flying and gave the General a migraine that would dog him for days.

He arrived at the *Hotel de la Paix* in Hotton a little after midnight, following two detours en route to consult with his superiors, Generals Courtney Hodges and Mathew Ridgway. His staff was already there, poring over maps spread out on tables in the dining room. Ridgway's instructions to Rose had been straightforward: he was to initiate intensive reconnaissance east from Hotton to find and engage the enemy. Ridgway left it to Rose to come up with a plan.

As he studied the maps in the early hours of December 20th, the situation was in such flux that Rose was unaware that Harvey Fraser's engineers were at that moment strapping 800 pounds of TNT and 300 pounds of satchel charges to the main abutment and three piers of the Hotton bridge, just 200 yards away. Nor was he aware that earlier in the evening Fraser's troops had arrested twenty-one men from a herd of civilians fleeing the village after an inspection of their baggage turned up American uniforms, cigarettes and rations. Presumably spies, they were transported to Namur for interrogation and possible execution.

* * *

COLONEL ROBERT "BOBBY" HOWZE CRUISED PAST THE prayer chapel on Barvaux Road marking the north entrance to Hotton at 0855, the village ahead reduced to silhouette beneath a blanket of fog. The 41-year old commanding officer of CCR was exhausted and bone-cold from the 15-hour march from Stolberg. Consistent with his instructions from Rose, half his troops had peeled off from the column north of Hotton to await further orders, while the bulk of his remaining forces coiled in a field on the outskirts of the village. With Howze was his headquarters company under the command of Captain John Anderson, which included the two-dozen men of CCR's Intelligence & Reconnaissance Platoon. An MP posted at the schoolhouse flagged the jeep to a halt, scrutinizing its occupants before directing them to the *Hotel de la Paix*, indicating a right turn at the bridge. Howze paused to survey the landscape. A thicket of trucks and half-tracks parked around the schoolhouse told him another unit, probably Division Headquarters Rear, had already claimed it for a command post. Across the street and cater-corner to the schoolhouse, a two-story farmhouse caught his eye.

Signaling to Anderson in the jeep behind him, he pointed to the farmhouse, then told his driver to proceed. A few minutes later he was standing in front of General Rose amidst a clattering of typewriters and clouds of stale cigarette smoke.

As always, Rose looked like he had just stepped from a parade, cleanly shaven, his olive-drab trousers bloused neatly into buffed cavalry boots. Returning Howze's salute, Rose inquired how he had fared during the march before turning to the maps spread out before them. His plan was simple but daring: three task forces would push east along roughly parallel routes to probe for the enemy, and to secure a 13-mile line from the town of Manhay southeast to Houffalize. Each task force, numbering approximately 500 men, would be comprised of reconnaissance troops in light tanks and armored cars, backed by a company of medium tanks and a battery of 105-mm howitzers. The task forces would be under the operational control of Colonel Prentiss Yeomans, whose reconnaissance troopers spearheaded each task force. Howze would exercise general control of the operation from an advance command post in Soy, behind the middle task force and three miles northeast of Hotton, where he would maintain a small reserve force of tanks and infantry. Rose's Headquarters Rear, located at the schoolhouse as Howze had guessed, would remain in Hotton until the next morning pending intelligence on the enemy, along with a section of wire and radio troops, elements of three companies of combat engineers, and Howze's own headquarters company. Rose's plan still required approval from General Ridgway, which he expected shortly. The briefing took fifteen minutes, or two Camels apiece for Rose and Howze.

Unlike Rose who had enlisted as a private and had shouldered his way almost invisibly up the career ladder, Howze descended from a distinguished line of West Pointers and had never known life outside of the Army. His mother's father, Brigadier General Hamilton Hawkins, had charged up San Juan Hill alongside Theodore Roosevelt. His father, Robert Howze, Sr., received the Medal of Honor in 1891 for his actions against the Sioux Nation at White River, South Dakota, later distinguishing himself in Cuba and in America's punitive expeditions to the Philippines and Mexico, where he gained fame for chasing Pancho Villa through the mountain passes of Chihuahua. Following his father's death in 1926, the Howze name was affixed seemingly everywhere: to the polo field at West Point, to the front gate at Fort Bliss, to an Army frigate, and the ultimate accolade, to his own Army base in Texas — Fort Howze. Rose was aware of his subordinate's impressive pedigree, having passed through Howze Gate countless times while stationed at Fort Bliss, and where, coincidentally, he had briefly pursued one Margaret "Peggy" Richmond, herself the daughter of a prominent cavalryman and the future Mrs. Howze. Rose approved of Howze's choice in women, but all that mattered now was how he comported himself in battle. On this the jury was still out as Howze was a relative newcomer to the war, having arrived in Europe in late September — after the brutal fighting in France and through the concrete-teeth of the Siegfried line.

Returning to the farmhouse he had chosen for his temporary command post, Howze found his Intelligence & Reconnaissance platoon huddled outside, its commander leaning against the building, his Thompson sub-machine gun slung over his shoulder. Calling him over, Howze saw that his top scout was sweating profusely and shivering. Both men knew this was a bad time to get sick, especially Howze, who intended that I&R would accompany him to Soy.

"You look lousy, lieutenant," he observed.

"I'm okay, colonel," said Mike McDonald.

Howze studied the scout's waxen face. Already a veteran of three battle campaigns, the 26 year-old New Yorker had proved himself a solid soldier. Howze relied on him to be his eyes and ears, sending him deep behind enemy lines to gather information, often by drawing fire. McDonald's reports were succinct and clear; he was agressive but not foolhardy; and he kept a cool head, an essential quality in any officer but critical for one leading men in combat. If Howze had any reservations about him at all, it was that he was too relaxed with his men, a leadership style antipodes apart from his own.

"This is what you'll do, lieutenant. You'll select a squad to remain here until further advised. The rest of your men will stand by to move with me. Then you will report to the aid-station, find a cot and sleep off that bug. Is that clear?"

Without realizing it, Bobby Howze had just made one of the luckier decisions he would make in the coming days.

Major General Maurice Rose (left), Lt. Colonel Harvey Fraser *(right)*.

Rose's Command Post, later used by John Wilson's signal company.

Colonel Robert "Bobby" Howze, Jr.

Major Charles Kapes, Chaplain John Kraka, and Lieutenant
Mike McDonald *(left to right)*. Stolberg, Germany — December 1944.

03

MAURICE ROSE'S THREE TASK FORCES PUSHED OFF IN SEARCH of the enemy around noon on the 20th. Task Force Kane was the furthest north; Task Force Tucker in the middle; and Task Force Hogan to the south. Once in position, the gap between each task force would be approximately four miles, covering an area of dense woods and bald hills streaked with a dozen winding roads. Of the three task force commanders, Lieutenant Colonel Sam Hogan was the most comfortable with his mission as he was protected on his right flank by the natural barrier of the Ourthe River, which allowed him to focus on what was to his front and left. None of them knew what to expect. As Hogan recalled, "Information of the enemy given to us was zero. This was only a little less than usual. However, the information of friendly troops given to us was also zero and this was quite a bit less than usual."

In Hotton, Howze organized his remaining infantry and tanks into a reserve task force under Lt. Colonel Bill Orr. He pressed Orr to shove off at 1300 hours, but pushed it back when informed that Orr was missing a platoon and still needed to gas up his vehicles. At 1425, Howze departed for Soy accompanied by a couple of message clerks, his liaison officer and half of Lt. McDonald's I&R platoon, commandeering a two-story stucco house in the center of the village for his command post. Orr's forces began arriving in Soy at 1530, and assembled in a barnyard up the street from Howze's CP.

By this time Task Force Hogan was in LaRoche. Their march route had taken them through the farmhouse villages of Melines, Trinal and Beffe, past a T-junction leading to the villages of Devantive and Samrée, and then through the hilltop village of Marcouray. They had seen no signs of the enemy. In LaRoche, Hogan was surprised to find supply and maintenance troops from the 7th Armored Division guarding the main road. Eager to be relieved after discouraging a probe by a German patrol, the soldiers all but kissed Hogan's men when they saw them. Hogan saw an opportunity to protect his rear flank and decided to keep them just where they were, but left two 105-mm howitzer crews to calm their nerves.

The road ahead wound through a steep twisting valley framed on one side by wooded cliffs and on the other by the Ourthe River. A mile west of Maboge, the column of 72 vehicles came to a sharp blind curve where it was stopped by a roadblock formed by several felled trees. The reconnaissance troopers on point climbed down from their light tank to inspect the obstacle. They decided it could not be cleared before nightfall and without broadcasting their presence to the enemy. Hogan reported the situation to Colonel Yeomens at 1630 hours. Yeomans ordered the task force to hold its position for the night, and directed Hogan to set up a command post in LaRoche.

Hogan chose for his CP one of the summer resort hotels overlooking the Ourthe. The lobby was littered with Christmas packages left there by Americans who had fled the city earlier in the day. Hogan claimed a couple of them, including one postmarked from his home state of Texas containing a fruitcake. A sergeant brought in a bedraggled officer who had been separated from his unit.

"Where in the world did you come from?" he asked Hogan. "Don't you realize you're cut off? The whole German Army is around this place!"

"Well," replied Hogan. "Here we are, and we have a good bit of firepower. If they want to run us out, we're ready for them."

* * *

AT 1645, GENERAL ROSE AND HIS STAFF GATHERED THEIR maps and typewriters and moved to the village of Erezée where Rose would be closer to the action. Left behind in Hotton and scattered everywhere were approximately 210 soldiers, along with dozens of trucks and other vehicles. On the north bank, some 70 men from the 143rd Signal Company occupied the buildings near the *Hotel de la Paix*; Bill Rodman had 35 men at the schoolhouse; another 40 men under John Anderson were across the street and at the *Fanfare Royale* aid-station; 35 men from the 23rd Engineers were in the houses along Soy Road near the bridge; and Charlie Kapes' half-dozen MPs were holed up at the Boiteaux fishing rod shop, taking turns checking the traffic for Germans posing as GIs. On the south bank, exposed to the biting cold, were 20 men from Harvey Fraser's 51st, their guns pointed across the river. From Rose's perspective, the most vital of these soldiers were his Signal company troops, which constituted the bulk of the Division's communications capability, including his entire telephone wire section, several powerful SCR 399 radios, and half his message center. Without them, he could communicate with Howze and his other commanders only by "small" radio, which had less range and was susceptible to interference in choppy terrain, severely hampering his message processing capability — the coding, transmitting, receiving, decoding and recording of messages.

Arriving in Erezée 15 minutes later, Rose could hear German artillery falling on Task Force Tucker in the vicinity of Amonines. Choosing the *Hotel de la Claire* for his advance CP, he radioed to his signal company and headquarters troops in Hotton to prepare to move out, though he didn't yet know where to send them. Soon the shelling subsided, causing Rose to radio that the move "probably" would not happen that night.

At 1730, a caravan of bridge trucks with another 150 men from the 23rd Engineers rolled into Hotton, accompanied by the 23rd's executive officer, Major Jack Fickessen. This brought the total troop-count in the village to nearly 360, the equivalent of two companies. Now dark with the temperature dropping, Americans could be found in every house and building on the north bank, crowding around fires, lying on floors, or, like Chaplain Kraka and his clerk, sprawled on a bed of potatoes in a cellar. Only the MPs manning check points on Barvaux Road and the unlucky few outposted to the eastern edge of the village to listen for the enemy were outside, shivering in the bone-chilling mist. To the extent the 3rd Armored troops were aware of Harvey Fraser's engineers on the other side of the bridge, stamping their feet around their weapons to keep warm, no one gave it much thought. The faint clap of artillery in the distance reassured them they were well to the rear, and in any event would be gone come morning.

This sense of relative safety was reinforced at 2000 hours

when a long column of trucks carrying troops from the 84th Infantry Division passed through Hotton, headlights blazing, en route to Marche. The commanding general of the 84th, Alexander Bolling, had come through an hour earlier. He had seen the jeeps, trucks and half-tracks parked everywhere, reflecting a substantial American presence in the village. Crossing the bridge, he questioned Fraser's gun crews, who reported things quiet and the bridge wired to blow. Bolling concluded that Hotton was secure.

He had left Palenburg, Germany, that morning, and like Rose the night before, had stopped in Werboment to get his orders from General Ridgway. The commander of the 18th Airborne Corps did not have much more to tell Bolling about the enemy's whereabouts than what he had told Rose, and his orders were similarly broad: the 84th would defend the area south of the Ourthe against attack from the east. Bolling understood this to mean that his troops were not to cross the Ourthe unless so ordered. Now, from what he had just seen, the 84th wasn't needed on the other side of the river.

Entering Marche, Bolling was confronted by a very different picture – "an atmosphere of panic" as it would later be described. The exodus of civilians fleeing to safety jammed the main roads out of the city. Some MPs stopped his jeep, then directed him to Fraser's CP.

"Are you by yourself, sir, or do you have any forces with you?" asked Fraser, who by now was so inured to the confusion nothing could surprise him.

"We have an infantry division on the road," said Bolling. "It will come in tonight."

Fraser's few men cheered the news like it was the announcement of the Second Coming, venting the strain that had gripped them for days. Bolling was impressed they were still there when everyone else had pulled out, but he was troubled that Fraser also had no information on the enemy beyond what was happening at Trois Ponts, some twenty miles away. Bolling decided to take a quick tour of the city to get his bearings. While doing so he stopped to speak with a young GI who told him that Hotton was in German hands. Bolling had just come from there and knew this wasn't the case. Nevertheless, he regarded the false report as "a vital piece of information" which, in the coming days, would cause him to discount the urgency of repeated calls for help from the troops in Hotton.

* * *

WHEN HE ARRIVED IN HOTTON IN THE EARLY EVENING OF December 20th, Jack Fickessen became the senior officer in the village. As a practical matter, this meant nothing to him or to the other ranking officers, who belonged to different units that just happened to be bivouacked there for the night. John Wilson, the commanding officer of the signal company troops, had never met Fickessen; Bill Rodman, in charge of Rose's headquarter troops parked at the schoolhouse, had never met him; and Howze's supply officer, John Anderson, knew Wilson but not the others. This was due to the sheer size of the 3rd Armored Division — some 15,000 troops at full strength — and because their units, with the exception of signal company, rarely interfaced. But the immediate reason no one saw a need to consult with each other, even to commiserate about the lousy weather, was because they all expected to be leaving Hotton soon.

Fickessen was not a popular figure inside the 23rd. While smart and physically imposing, the Texas A&M graduate had a patronizing and brusque manner that grated on just about everyone. Even his fellow officers regarded him as a bit too Texan for their taste, twinging at his tendency to bark orders when a simple command would suffice. Yet liked or not, they all agreed he got things done.

49

Fickessen settled into a home midway down Soy Road, where he found some junior officers feeding lumps of coal into an iron stove. Tired and hungry from his long day of travel, he peppered them with questions concerning the status of their troops and equipment, their readiness to move out, what they had seen and heard, and whether a listening post had been established. Satisfied that things were in order, he wolfed down a can of C-rations consisting of the usual mystery meat, beans, dry biscuits, and a piece of hard candy. Then he dragged himself to an empty corner and went to sleep.

* * *

UP AT THE SCHOOLHOUSE, CAPTAIN BILL RODMAN was eavesdropping on a bull session with a cluster of enlisted men, smiling at their banter. Instinct told him things were about to heat up, and he wanted his men to be mentally rested before it happened. The 26 year-old college dropout had already made his rounds to make sure they had double-checked their weapons, had plenty of ammo, and knew what to do if his hunch played out. Rodman couldn't resist. His temperament was that of a coach, part teacher and part disciplinarian, supportive but firm, and above all protective of his players. His men respected him.

Rodman's job at Division Headquarters Rear – call name Omaha Rear – was to maintain the Division's voluminous records documenting everything from procurement to personnel. It was an endlessly dry task that generated truckloads of paper and little opportunity for glory, hardly what the adventure-seeking Rodman had envisioned on enlistment. When the Division moved, everything moved with it: tankers and infantry out front; signal company and combat engineers behind them; and everyone else – maintenance and supply, medical company, and headquarters personnel – in the rear where they were less likely to get killed. Still, these rear-guard troops occasionally found themselves ducking shells and dodging snipers. The previous August, Rodman led a patrol to capture two Germans seen prowling in the vicinity. The patrol killed four and returned with 86 prisoners. Cited for "using smart, soldierly tactics," Rodman was awarded a Bronze Star. Since then he had privately yearned for more action.

The son of a prominent Philadelphia surgeon, Rodman had attended the prestigious Phillips Exeter Academy where he had captained the track team and was the only student in the school's history to sport a tattoo. He liked to brag that he had two of them, but in truth the first was really a self-inflicted scar he'd gotten from branding the letters "RL" on his forearm with a red-hot clothes hanger. The "R" stood for Rodman and the "L" for Longmaid, the last name of his two best friends — brothers Dave and John — who similarly disfigured themselves in a teen-age pact of loyalty. Disappointed when the letters receded beneath dark summer tans, the three friends drove to a Philadelphia parlor where they acquired identical tattoos depicting a musketeer's sword piercing a star. According to Rodman, the image "signified that we would always reach for the stars."

From Exeter he enrolled at the University of Pennsylvania, barely squeaking through his freshman year before taking a job as a runner and copy boy at the *Philadelphia Evening Bulletin*. The Longmaid boys went on to Yale, keeping in close touch with Rodman until 1940 when the three of them enlisted together. From there they split up. Having grown up around horses, Rodman wanted to be in cavalry; Anglophile Dave chose air reconnaissance so he could save Britain; and John joined the Army Air Corps. Three months later John was killed in a training crash, a loss Rodman would never get over.

Like Fickessen, Rodman saw no reason to confer with the other officers in the village. He doubted things would heat up *in* Hotton, yet he followed standard operating procedure and set up a listening post at the prayer chapel on Barvaux Road. Around midnight he stirred from a catnap and ventured out into the cold to personally check that his men were alert.

* * *

ACROSS THE STREET, CAPTAIN JOHN ANDERSON WAS catching up on paperwork. His job was to see to it that the 2,500 enlisted men and 120 officers of the 36th Armored Infantry Regiment had everything they needed to fight the war. Since its baptism of fire in the hedgerows of Normandy, the 36th had been engaged in virtually constant combat, with casualties — killed, wounded and missing in action — averaging fully ten percent of the regiment's strength monthly. Even Chaplain Kraka had been hit, his back and shoulders ripped open by shrapnel, some of which he still carried with him. Anderson had experienced the nightmare of enemy (and friendly) bombing and shelling — St. Lo was the worst — but he had been spared the horror of close-up combat. Not once had he reached for the .45-caliber pistol he carried on his hip, or the .30 caliber carbine stowed in his jeep. In fact, the only Germans Anderson had seen were dead or prisoners, which suited him fine. He was, after all, a supply officer, and in Howze's opinion a very capable one.

A native of Spartanburg, South Carolina, and the grandson of a Confederate general, the soft-spoken Anderson had sung in the Glee Club at Wofford College where he majored in French, then taught second grade before enlisting. He looked like a teacher, too, tall and good-postured with the quiet authority of one accustomed to having the last word. The enlisted men viewed him as square, an impression informed by the fact that he didn't drink, smoke or swear, attributes that landed him in the smallest minority of soldiers now at war. His fellow officers saw him much the same way, though with them he loosened up, crooning corny tunes and flashing his homespun Southern wit. No one appreciated him more than Phil Zulli, the 36th's gregarious recreation officer, who delighted in ribbing Anderson about his fastidious ways. They had known each other since 1941 at Fort Benning, where the playful, chain-smoking Zulli adopted the habit of lighting his cigarettes from Anderson's Zippo. By the time they reached England, it seemed to Anderson that he was lighting all of Zulli's cigarettes. Finally, he just gave him the lighter. Zulli returned it a week later with an engraved message of thanks, then promptly resumed hitting on Anderson whenever he needed a light.

On the night of December 20th, Anderson strolled to the *Fanfare Royale* aid-station to check on his friend. Zulli was asleep, as was Mike McDonald in the cot next to him, both dead to the world despite the drone of trucks from General Bolling's 84th rolling toward Marche. He passed time talking to one of the doctors, then returned to his CP. It did not occur to him that in less than twelve hours he would be standing on the front line of the war.

Captains Phil Zulli,
Bill Rodman, and
John Anderson
*(clockwise from
top left).*

04.

TEN MILES AWAY, TASK FORCE TUCKER WAS TAKING A POUND-ing from *Kampfgruppe* Bayer of the *116th Panzer Division.* Known as the *Greyhound* for its swift movement in battle, the 116th had been formed in early 1944 from the battered rem-nants of several armored divisions lifted from the Russian front in order to meet the long anticipated Allied invasion of France. Three quarters of its 13,500 men had seen action in the East, and with the 116th had participated in every major campaign on the western front, sustaining massive losses of personnel and equipment while forging a reputation second to none in the German Panzer Corps. Recently refitted with new tanks and young replacements, its officers and senior enlisted men were among the most experienced combat soldiers in Europe.

The grand strategy behind the German counter-offensive had been laid out in a highly classified memorandum titled "Di-rectives for Battle Conduct:"

> The objective is the encirclement of the 21st Army Group and the Ninth and First American Armies by a quick assault on Antwerp . . . . The pre-requisite for the success of this operation is to sur-prise the enemy, which requires <u>secrecy, speed, and mobility – everything must be subordinated to these.</u> (Emphasis in original.)

The port of Antwerp on the Belgium coast was the Allies'

largest and closest supply point to the German front, and thus essential to prosecuting the war. If Antwerp fell again under German control, then all supplies would have to be trucked in from Normandy, hundreds of miles to the south, greatly slowing the Allied advance. By Hitler's reasoning, retaking Antwerp would extend the war longer than the Americans had the stomach to fight, presenting him with an opportunity to sue for peace from a position of strength. This, in turn, would enable him to concentrate his dwindling resources against the Russians bearing down on him from the north and east. Everything hinged on capturing Antwerp, and killing as many Americans as possible in the process.

To get to Antwerp, the German Armies had to cross the largest river in Belgium, the Meuse, beyond which the rolling terrain was open to the coast. But to reach the Meuse they first had to get through the Ardennes, which meant crossing several smaller rivers such as the Ourthe that flowed mostly north-south. There were good roads leading west on which the attacking forces could move, but everything depended upon crossing these smaller rivers. It was essential to move quickly through key road centers such as Bastogne and St. Vith, and to capture bridges like those at Trois Pont and Hotton undamaged. Speed of movement was critical, not only for the surprise element of the plan, but to gain as much ground as possible before the weather cleared and Allied planes returned to the skies, which they controlled. Pockets of resistance were to be by-passed in order to keep moving.

Now in his fifth day of continuous fighting, *Oberst* (Colonel) Johannes Bayer still had 21 battle-worthy tanks — fifteen

PzKpfw V Panthers and six PzKpfw IVs — also known as Mk IVs — supported by a battalion each of *Panzer-Grenadiers* (armored infantry) and towed artillery, two platoons of tank destroyers, and a company of combat engineers to sweep mines and repair bridges. Bayer's exact troop count on the night of December 20th is unknown, but he probably still had about 2,500 men. Earlier in the evening, Bayer knocked out eight American tanks in the vicinity of Samrée, where he also captured an American supply dump holding 26,000 gallons of precious fuel and 15,000 food rations. For Bayer it was found treasure. Drivers hurriedly fueled their vehicles, then loaded up as many gas cans as they could carry. A little before midnight, he ordered a task force under Major Gerhard Tebbe to swing southwest to seize the bridge at Hotton. Tebbe's march route took him through the villages of Devantive, Beffe, Trinal and the hamlet of Melines, just downhill from Soy and a mile from Hotton as the crow flies. Significantly, Task Force Hogan had taken much of the same route to LaRoche just twelve hours earlier.

At 0430 on December 21st, John Anderson reported hearing vehicles moving to his south. "South" to Howze meant Marche, so he assumed the movement was the 84th Infantry Division still settling in. An hour later, a patrol reported being fired upon by Germans in an American vehicle near the village of Wy, a short distance through the woods from Melines. Howze wasn't overly alarmed by this report either since Wy, located in the zone between Task Force Hogan and Task Force Tucker (now reinforced and operating as Task Force Orr), was presumably cut off to the enemy. Nevertheless, he sent word to organize a platoon to investigate the report.

The report was accurate, and the American vehicle, captured in Samrée the night before, was part of Gerhardt Tebbe's task force now in Melines. When he arrived there around 0500, Tebbe promptly sent out patrols to reconnoiter the area. In addition to the one in Wy just northeast of his position, he sent a patrol to Hotton, and dispatched four tanks to the village of Hampteau with orders to secure the footbridge across the Ourthe or to destroy it if it was defended. The previous day, Harvey Fraser's engineers had wired the bridge to blow, leaving a three-man squad on the south bank armed with a .50 caliber machine gun and a bazooka. Still pitch dark and foggy, the engineers only heard the tanks as they approached the bridge and opened fire. The German tankers saw the muzzle flash and replied with three rounds, at least one of which hit the bridge causing it to sag into the river. Disinclined to press their luck, Fraser's men took off on foot down LaRoche Road for Hotton.

At 0615 hours, a 22-man platoon from the 23rd Engineers under Lieutenant Edmund Socha departed for Melines to investigate the report of shots fired on the American patrol. Melines consisted of several farmhouses and a grain mill clustered around two road junctions. From Soy the village could be reached by two routes. The most direct was via a narrow road that dipped straight downhill. The other way was down Soy Road to the *Quatre Bras* road junction, a distance of about a mile, and from there downhill another half-mile to Melines. Socha's platoon shoved off in single column along the first route, armed with rifles and trailed by a radio-equipped jeep. The patrol reached Melines about 0645. Finding nothing, they continued south a few hundred yards toward a wide hogback hill known as *La Roumière*. Socha was behind the lead scout, Corporal John Shields. He heard tracked vehicles approaching as Shields signaled the platoon to halt.

Two days earlier, the 31-year old Shields had mailed a letter home in which he lauded the relative comforts of Stolberg: the hot shower, a change of clothes, a real meal. He also had just missed drawing a pass to Paris. "My name was third but only two could go. Maybe I can go after the 1st of the year." Now the murky darkness erupted in machine gun fire. Socha saw Shields dart for a ditch below a tall hedgerow where "he was not seen by anyone again."

Had Socha been able to slow things down and in better light, he would have seen Shields empty the eight-round clip in his M-1 Garand rifle in the direction of the tracer rounds hissing past him, then reach for a grenade at the same moment a bullet slammed into his chest, spinning him around and throwing him face down in the ditch, the first casualty in the defense of Hotton.

A Panther tank appeared in the field above the spot where Shields had fallen. The tank tipped down the hedgerow directly over the lifeless soldier, burying his corpse in the Belgian mud and nearly colliding with a German half-track – most likely an *SdKfz 250* or *251*. The half-track flanked by grenadiers advanced in Socha's direction, sweeping the road with machine gun fire but miraculously missing him except for a bullet crease to the heel of one boot. Pinned down and outgunned, Socha surrendered his platoon. Six of his men had been killed and an unknown number wounded in the space of a few terrifying minutes.

Socha later would write that he was separated from the other prisoners and taken to "a short, dumpy colonel" who greeted him with a smile. "I see you come. I vait." This almost certainly was Johannes Bayer. A junior officer put a pistol to Socha's temple and demanded to know the number and location of Sherman tanks in Hotton. The question was prompted by a reconnaissance report of a significant American presence in the village, though no tanks had been spotted. Bayer ordered the officer to stand down, then led Socha to a staff car accompanied by two guards. Together they squeezed past Tebbe's column climbing the steep road to Quatre Bras, turned on Soy Road and entered the *Sur les Hys* woods above Hotton. Socha watched as German tanks and mortar crews deployed along the ridgeline, unsure why he had been brought there. Then he was taken away for interrogation.

Around 0730, a farmer entered the Hotton schoolhouse sputtering French and pointing to the east. "Les Boches! Les Boches!" Bill Rodman heard the commotion and came over. He had forgotten most of his Exeter French but the farmer's words ("The Germans! The Germans!) registered instantly. Before he could slap himself on the back the low sky above Hotton began raining mortar fire. One round opened the schoolhouse roof, rocking the building. Four men in the attic caught in the explosion of wood and tile rushed for the stairs.

Down by the river, Woody Williams was flipping pancakes behind the *Hotel de la Paix* when his mess truck was showered with earth, brick and glass. Known as "Fancy Woody" for his habit of drinking coffee from a cup rather a mess can, he couldn't believe what he was seeing. Everywhere he looked men were scrambling about like extras in a Buster Keaton movie, throwing themselves into doorways for cover, racing to find their platoons and clinging to any familiar face. Mike McDonald flew from his cot at the *Fanfare Royale* aid-station instantly cured of his pneumonia. Lacing his boots, he dashed to Anderson's CP to collect his squad. He saw Chaplain Kraka standing outside and looking up as though contemplating the weather. "C'mon, Father, inside." For once the priest listened to him. McDonald was not unnerved; he had experienced worse, and had long accepted that it was only a matter of time before he met the bullet or shell with his name on it.

The first order of business was to locate the enemy. Huddling briefly with his men, he sent them fanning out through the village. "Find that mortar and take it out," he said to two of them. "Tabby, you and Randle see what's cookin' at the river."

At 0805, Fickessen radioed the commanding officer of the 23rd Engineers that Hotton was being shelled, who relayed the report to General Rose's command post. Rose immediately summoned Colonel Howze to Erezée, who arrived ten minutes later. It was obvious to both men that the enemy would not be shelling Hotton unless they thought Americans were there. The big question was where the fire was coming from. Fickessen's message said the village was being "shelled," which generally referred to artillery that could strike targets from a distance of several miles. Mortar fire, on the other hand, had an effective range of less than a mile. Howze had not heard any of the battle noise in Hampteau or Melines due to the terrain and heavy fog. Adding to the uncertainty was the troubling fact that Socha's patrol had not reported back.

Al Camurati and Roy Luff, meanwhile, were standing on the railroad embankment between the schoolhouse and the orchard when they saw a crouched figure in a gray overcoat approaching them in short dashes. Notwithstanding that mortar rounds were dropping all around them, Camurati persuaded himself that the person coming toward them was an old woman out for a morning stroll. "You're crazy, it's a Kraut!" said Luff as the ground under their boots broke up in fist-sized chunks of earth. Without further conversation they tumbled down the embankment and raced to Fickessen's CP, dodging cattle as they ran.

By 0820, Fickessen had formed two 12-man squads, directing one to set up a defensive line along the railroad embankment, and the other to check the houses on Soy Road. He also set two roadblocks, parking a bridge truck at the old grain mill where the road narrowed to a width of just 16 feet, and positioning a supply truck in the road closer to the bridge. What he had not done was check to see what was inside the truck. Had anyone done so, they would have found that it was loaded to the tarp with explosives. This was tantamount to placing gasoline next to a stove.

Howze was back in Soy at 0830 when Fickessen, now acting commander of the 3rd Armored troops in Hotton, reported that the village was under attack by mortar and automatic weapons fire. Howze was flabbergasted. The Germans were there. He raced outside with his liaison officer and together they sped off by jeep toward Hotton to confirm the report. They stopped at a curve in the road below the village where there was line-of-sight to the *Quatre Bras* road junction. Howze peered through binoculars into the lifting fog. Sure enough, a column of vehicles from Melines was turning south on Soy Road.

"Christ!" he bellowed. "Where'd they come from?" The two officers stared in disbelief as the column snaked toward Hotton. They heard the faint staccato pop of automatic weapons emanating from the village. "Go find us some help," said Howze.

While his liaison officer sped off toward Erezée, John Bonner and two others from Fickessen's hastily assembled reconnaissance squad were checking the last houses on Soy Road. They could hear shooting on the other side of the railroad embankment, but they had seen no Germans. In the first house they encountered a man with a small girl. The six-foot-four Bonner was struck by the girl's clean white dress, as though she were heading to church. The girl's father pleaded with them in broken English not to fire their weapons from his home, fearing the Germans would destroy it. As the Americans had yet to see any enemy, they readily complied. The next house was empty. Entering the last house they found several civilians squeezed together in the living room, all understandably agitated. "Don't worry," said Bonner. "It's okay. We're here. It'll be alright." Mounting the stairs to the second floor the soldiers heard an engine start, and looking out a back window saw a German tank.

"I don't believe I touched three steps on my way down," Bonner recalled, describing his exit from the house. "I've often wondered what they thought of the recently calm, collected GI as he was beating a hasty retreat."

At the Verdin house on the other side of the railroad embankment, Ken Doncaster and "Lute" Kuhn were shooting from a second floor window at grenadiers crouched beside another tank when they came under fire from the railroad embankment, their own men mistaking them for Germans. Scuttling downstairs they found the living room engulfed in flames, briefly considered hiding in the cellar, then jumped from a window practically landing on the grenadiers they had been shooting at a moment earlier. Disarmed, they were taken to an armored car parked behind the *Chapel des Anges* prayer hut. A dead German soldier was laid out on the hood. He appeared to Doncaster to be little more than a boy. Ordered onto the fenders, they were whisked uphill for interrogation. The first question put to Doncaster was whether he knew a Lieutenant Socha. He shook his head no, but his eyes belied him. For Gerhardt Tebbe, this confirmed he was with the 23rd, and collaborated an earlier scouting report that Hotton was held by rear-guard troops. Taking this village, he thought, will be a walk in the country.

As prisoners of war, Doncaster and Kuhn would endure frostbite and starvation while filling holes created by allied bombers. Subsisting on a diet of gruel and hard bread, Doncaster would drop forty-five pounds by the time he regained his freedom.

* * *

THE SITUATION IN HOTTON WENT FROM BAD TO WORSE when, at 0928, Fickessen reported four enemy tanks moving near the connector road. Two minutes later, Lt. McDonald radioed from an attic window at the schoolhouse; he counted five tanks.

"Can you still see down there?" said Howze.

"I can still see business down there."

"Maintain observation and if you can, push forward."

By this time Howze was receiving calls left and right. Anderson chimed in at 0947: "Rear CP being attacked by seven tanks."

"Handle as best you can," Howze answered.

"That's what we are doing."

At 0955, Fickessen radioed that the four enemy tanks reported earlier were coming his way. "Holding out as best we can, house to house proposition."

Two of the tanks bearing down on the 23rd's position along Soy Road were Panthers — fifty-ton behemoths armed with a long-barrel 75-mm gun and three 7.92-mm machine guns. Reaching the first roadblock at the grain mill, the lead Panther pushed the bridge truck back and to the side like it was a toy. As it did so it entered the gun sights of the 51st Engineers across the river, who unleashed a torrent of fire from their 40-mm *Bofors* and .50-caliber machine guns, joined by a 37-mm gun manned by an ad hoc crew from the 23rd and 51st. Ferocious as it was, the concentrated fire did not damage the tank. Inside the Panther's cramped compartment, however, it sounded like a hundred blacksmiths hammering simultaneously on the same anvil. The intense fire nonetheless dissuaded the grenadiers escorting the tank from showing themselves, and they took cover in the houses. Without infantry the tanks were basically blind, and vulnerable to assault by shoulder-fired bazooka rockets. Seeing that the lead tank was unprotected, the second Panther and the smaller Mk IV's behind it abandoned Soy Road altogether, slipping into the orchard behind the houses. Here the grenadiers found themselves taking fire from Americans positioned atop the railroad embankment, causing them to also seek cover in the houses. Suddenly all the houses on the eastern end of Soy Road were occupied by Germans.

A little earlier, Bill Rodman had paid Fickessen a visit. He had found two straggler tanks from the Stolberg march — an early model Sherman and a Stuart light tank — neither of which, Rodman conceded, stood much of a chance against a Panther. "Get 'em down here," Fickessen told him. Now the 13-ton Stuart, with its mere inch-and-a-half of armor and 37-mm "pea shooter," dutifully started east on Soy Road in full view of the lead Panther. For the crew inside the Stuart this was a bowel-loosening sight; they bailed out an instant before the Panther fired, lifting the light tank into the air and setting it afire. The Panther swung its gun toward the engineers firing from across the river. As it did so, the Sherman emerged from an alley beside the Dirette home, 50 yards from the bridge, and fired two rounds at the Panther. The German crew felt like they'd been hit by a pair of speeding *Volkswagens,* loud jolting thuds but ultimately harmless. This was due not only to the Panther's thick armor, but also to the high-angle front glacis plate that aided in deflecting the rounds. The Panther replied with a single armor-piercing round that penetrated the Sherman's box-like front like a knife through butter, exiting out the rear. Miraculously, none of the crew was killed. Then, swinging its gun a few degrees left, the Panther fired at the supply-truck roadblock. The explosives-laden truck detonated like a bomb, disintegrating the truck and blowing out most of the windows on both sides of the river.

Although less than a hundred yards from the bridge and with the road ahead open, the Panther now backed up. John Bonner had been shooting down at the tank from a window hoping to ignite one of the gas cans strapped atop the hull. Deciding he might have better luck outside, the 21 year-old Philadelphian raced downstairs and scurried out the back door. What he saw next stunned him: crawling toward him was a GI whose nose and part of his cheek bones had been shot off. Sickened by the profuse amount of blood, the dazed Bonner lifted the faceless soldier to his feet and led him toward Barvaux Road.

The Panther came to a grinding halt alongside the Bay family home. According to a later account by the 51st Engineers, they then fired 16 rounds from the 37-mm gun in three minutes, disabling the tank by targeting its bogie wheels and track. Veterans from the 23rd claimed the tank was stopped by a bazooka round fired by one of their own. Whatever the truth or amalgamation of truths, all agreed the turret hatch flew open and the German crew attempted to bail out. All four crew members were shot at close range. At 1000 hours — incredibly, just five minutes after reporting that enemy tanks were "coming this way" — Fickessen radioed Howze that the first Panther had been knocked out.

Johannes Bayer would not learn the nature of his tankers' wounds until that night. Because certain of the crew had been killed by headshots, Bayer concluded it was the work of "sharpshooters," causing him to question Tebbe's assessment that Hotton was defended by rear-guard troops.

* * *

IN THE ORCHARD, the commanders of the other tanks decided to breach the wall bordering Barvaux Road and secure the bridge from the north. As Providence would have it, a new-model Sherman from an unknown unit appeared on the south bank seemingly out of nowhere. The M4 Sherman was a huge improvement over its predecessor M3, firing a slightly larger round (76-mm) through a longer gun tube at a much higher muzzle velocity (2,650 feet per second). It was also heavier due to a full three inches of armor, slightly less than the Panther. By comparison, the Panther fired a 75-mm round that traveled much faster, about 3,300 feet per second, giving it significantly greater penetration capability than the new Sherman. Despite these improvements, the Sherman's best chance of winning a duel was to hit the Panther's side at close range without getting shot first.

An officer from the 51st coaxed the stray tank into a firing position just back from the bridge on Marche Road where it was partially shielded by a house. The Panther, commanded by *Oberleutnant* (Lieutenant) Köhn, crashed the wall and turned south, less than 100 yards from the bridge. The Sherman fired, the round ricocheting off the Panther's front glacis plate. A couple of Fraser's engineers were at that moment wading chest deep in the river repairing the detonation wires to the explosives under the bridge. They heard a violent whoosh as the shell passed overhead, the sound akin to a speeding train emerging from a tunnel. The Panther did not return fire, probably because it could not see the Sherman.

Köhn and his crew certainly felt the blow, but equally troubling was the steady ping of rifle fire, which told them that their infantry had abandoned them. Köhn decided to retreat to the orchard just as the two Mk IVs crashed the wall. Seeing the Panther retreat, the smaller tanks also pulled back to the orchard. The three tanks idled there briefly, either discussing or unsure what to do. The Panther started east toward the *Sur les Hys* woods hugging the backs of the houses on Soy Road for cover.

According to the 51st Engineers, an unidentified soldier approached one of their officers at the bridge.

"Captain, I'll flush out that tank over there."

"Well, boy, go ahead," the officer replied.

The soldier crossed the bridge with a bazooka and ducked behind a building. There was an explosion, and a moment later the Panther's hull appeared in a narrow alley between two homes. The Sherman saw it and fired, this time piercing the Panther's side-armor. A shower of incandescent steel fragments filled the tank's fighting compartment, taking out one of Köhn's eyes and killing three of his crew. The Mk IVs had seen enough and fled the orchard for the nearby hills.

Soldiers from the 3rd Armored remembered things differently, claiming this Panther was also stopped by bazooka fire. The kill was credited to various men including Charlie Kapes, who later was treated for burns to his neck and cheek from the blowback as the rocket exited the tube. Hearing the story later, Mike McDonald could not resist ribbing his friend. "Ah hell," said Kapes. "How was I supposed to know where to stand? I never fired one of those things before!"

At 1100, Fickessen radioed Howze that the attack had been stopped.

Just over an hour had elapsed since the first Panther appeared on Soy Road. During this time, John Anderson had sent a stream of confusing and frantic messages to Soy. At 1007, he radioed that enemy tanks were "entering town." Howze questioned whether these tanks were in addition to, and distinct from, those reported by Anderson, Fickessen and McDonald an hour earlier.

"From what direction are those guys coming? Are they coming from the east?"

"Tanks entering town from the south," said Anderson.

Once again, south to Howze meant they were coming from across the river.

"Tell me if that column is from the east or from the south."

"Attack is coming from southeast."

At 1035, Anderson had radioed: "Situation desperate. Is help coming?" Five minutes later he radioed again. "Is help coming?"

"YES," answered Howze.

At 1115 — fifteen minutes after Fickessen reported that the attack had been stopped — the supply officer radioed that the situation was "still desperate." While Howze pondered why two officers so close to each other were seeing the situation so differently, Fickessen reported that a small task force had arrived and was "starting to push the enemy out of the town." It was the first good news Howze had heard all morning. Thirty-five minutes later, a much-relieved Anderson sent word that "friendly troops have moved into town."

That it had taken Anderson so long to learn that help had arrived — indeed, had passed within spitting distance of his

70

CP — highlighted the dearth of communication between and among the various units in the village. Howze knew this had to be rectified immediately. It was imperative that everyone knew what everyone else was doing.

* * *

SECOND LIEUTENANT JACK WARDEN HAD RECEIVED HIS BATtlefield commission six days earlier, following a vicious fight near the Ruhr River that wiped out half his company, including the bulk of then Sergeant Warden's platoon. The 21 year-old Texan had a reputation as "a real good combat man." The tribute boiled down to an ability to manage fear under fire. "You just needed to think about doing your job and getting it done," Warden recalled. "Do your job and somebody lives a little bit longer. And when everyone's doing the same thing, well, it works out pretty well."

On the morning of December 21st, Warden's 18-man platoon was posted on a roadblock in Ny, another wisp of a village near Soy. With him were four medium tanks under Lieutenant Bill Smithers. Around 1000 hours, a voice crackled from Smithers' radio asking for the "Dough leader." Smithers handed the radio hand-set to Warden.

"Beer Three," said Warden, identifying himself as B Company, Third Platoon.

"Go to Hotton," said the voice. "Friends in trouble."

A quick glance at Smithers' map revealed that Hotton was three miles southwest of their position. The two officers formed into a column with Warden on point in his half-track, followed by two Shermans, a second half-track carrying the rest of Warden's men, and the two other tanks pulling up the rear. At Barvaux Road the column turned south, entering Hotton at 1115. Warden headed straight for the smoke, where he counted four dead tanks, two German and two American, and saw the still burning heap of metal that had been the supply truck road-block. Someone pointed out a building across the river where Fickessen had moved his command post. Informed that Germans occupied some of the houses along Soy Road, Smithers staggered his tanks between the bridge and the sawmill above the schoolhouse, while Warden's platoon began the arduous task of clearing the houses.

With the arrival of Warden's task force, Fickessen was ordered to release the 23rd's bridge company, together with a section of John Wilson's signal company. This reduced the troop count on the north bank to about 200 men, but between Warden's platoon and McDonald's I&R squad, there were now thirty combat soldiers in the village along with four tanks. Doctors at the Fanfare Royale aid-station also took advantage of the lull in the fighting to evacuate the most seriously wounded. At 1130, two ambulance trucks started north for Barvaux. They got as far as the sawmill when they came under attack by mortar and machine guns causing both trucks to leave the road, one of them flipping over. At the schoolhouse, Rodman's men witnessed what had happened and raced to help, pulling the dazed and wounded from the trucks and helping them back to the aid-station. Rodman only heard about the incident. Like everyone else, he was incensed by the attack as the trucks' side panels were clearly marked with red crosses. "You weren't supposed to shoot at those guys," said Rodman. "It reminded us why we were over there in the first place."

At 1310, General Rose informed Howze that Bolling's 84th would relieve the forces in Hotton that afternoon. Rose obviously had communicated with General Ridgway, to whom Bolling also reported, and therefore had every reason to assume that Bolling had been told the same thing. Colonel Howze relayed the news to Fickessen and Anderson.

"From what direction?" said Anderson. "Are friendly troops approaching town from the south?"

Howze got back to him at 1700. "Location of friendly force not known. They will approach your position from southwest." At 1730, a depleted platoon arrived at the bridge. Anderson's radio message hardly masked his disappointment.

"Friendly troops that came in were about fifteen men."

"Friendly troops expected anytime," answered Howze. "When they arrive our task force will be relieved and moved to new assembly area. You will remain where you are to await further instructions."

Harvey Fraser recalled that twenty men showed up at the bridge, about the same number he had posted there. Fraser assumed that because the Germans had not renewed their attack that they had been scared off, and thus viewed the fresh troops as relief for his own men. He ordered most of them back to Marche, maintaining a skeleton crew in the unlikely event it became necessary to blow the bridge. In his mind, Hotton had been saved and the 51st had saved it.

Although Fickessen and Anderson would have preferred to see the entire 84th Infantry Division on their side of the bridge, in fact their situation was much improved. At 1530, Fickessen had called a meeting of the officers in charge of the various units, and for the first time everyone knew who else was in the village, where they were, and what they had to fight with. They took stock: except for the medics, every man (including Chaplain Kraka) had either a rifle or pistol or both; they had two-dozen trucks, half-tracks and jeeps mounted with .50 caliber or .30 caliber machine guns; and there was an abundance of ammunition. In addition, McDonald had found an 81-mm mortar crew with 150 high-explosive (HE) rounds and flares. The 81-mm mortar was a devastating anti-personnel weapon, its HE round packed with lead pellets that had a killing radius of about 20 yards, greater than that if the ground was hard or frozen. And they had tanks.

But they had something else everyone had overlooked, which now would play a pivotal role in the defense of Hotton. At the *Hotel de la Paix*, John Wilson's signal company was sitting on enough telephones and line to wire a small town, replete with a switchboard. Once a communications net was laid down, everyone could talk to each other in real time. The exception was Howze. Because the Germans occupied the high ground between Hotton and Soy, it was impossible to run a phone line to him. He still could only communicate by radio, but at least he knew they were talking to each other in Hotton, which perhaps would eliminate the confusion of that morning.

With nightfall an hour away, the Americans went to work. The signal company troops ran wire. Fickessen and Warden disbursed their men in the houses overlooking the orchard, and set up a four-man observation post on the bluff above LaRoche

Road. Rodman and Anderson supervised the placement of men and machine guns between the east-facing buildings above the railroad embankment, including 35 men in and around the sawmill and another fifteen at the prayer hut on Barvaux Road. McDonald deployed his squad at strategic points in the village, establishing his mortar observation post in the schoolhouse. By dusk the defense was in place.

Rodman was thrilled there were "real soldiers" in the village, particularly McDonald, whom he probably recognized from Officer Candidates School at Fort Knox, where they had graduated in the same class on July 4, 1942. While still light, McDonald ordered up a smoke round to adjust his mortar fire, targeting the cemetery where he knew there were grenadiers. The range was good but it was too far north. "Right one-hundred," he said to the mortar crew. A moment later: "Use HE and traverse and search." Several rounds arched silently inside the stone walls of the cemetery. McDonald and Rodman heard the distant screams and saw movement. "He knew how to put those shells to good use," Rodman recalled. "It was a beautiful sight. We kept saying 'Thank God, oh God, we love you!'"

The flat terrain of the village gave the Americans a distinct defensive advantage, at least north of the railroad embankment where, except for a few farmhouses, it was mostly open field up to the woods. An attack on the schoolhouse and sawmill required that the enemy expose themselves, first to mortar and then to the machine gun fire from Barvaux Road. Only night offered an attacking force any real cover. McDonald knew he would have to use his few flares sparingly.

When darkness came and the temperature fell below

freezing, Howze put the village under blackout, instructing Charlie Kapes to keep civilians off the streets. John Anderson continued to send messages regarding the whereabouts of the expected relief. Howze's frustration came through. "Our mission is to hold Hotton until relieved by the 84th . . . . hold that place at all cost." The shelling gradually subsided. At 2110, Anderson radioed that it was "all quiet outside," adding that it was "rather light tonight." Across the river, Jack Fickessen used the quiet to tally their losses: 23 men had been wounded and eight were missing. His figures did not include the 22 men from Socha's platoon killed or captured that morning, or Harvey Fraser's two wounded at the bridge.

* * *

THAT MORNING SAM HOGAN RECEIVED ORDERS TO REPORT to Colonel Yeomans in Grandmenil at 0800. The 29-year old West Pointer got off to a late start because his jeep radio had been left on all night, draining the jeep's battery and requiring a jump before he could leave. Accompanying him to the meeting were his executive officer Major Walker, his reconnaissance officer Clark Worrell, Hogan's orderly and two drivers. Their route would be the same one Hogan's task force had taken the day before. The two jeeps passed through Marcouray and were approaching the T-junction leading to the villages of Devantive and Samrée, about a mile east of Beffe, when they came upon two American half-tracks and a jeep parked in the middle of the road. Standing around the vehicles eating K-rations were about twenty men, all but two of whom were dressed in GI uniforms. Hogan assumed they were American with two prisoners. Clark Worrell in the second jeep realized it was an enemy roadblock. "Back up, Colonel!" he yelled. "They're Germans!" Hogan's driver stalled their jeep shifting into reverse, by which time the Germans were shooting at them. Hogan's party – less the driver of the second jeep – took to the woods alongside the road, the German troops in pursuit, while the driver escaped down the road where he was later picked up by an American medic jeep. They returned to LaRoche and reported Hogan's party as missing.

Hogan with his driver and orderly had run a couple hundred yards when they came to an open field. Walker and Worrell saw them and came over. Huffing for breath as bullets clipped the trees around them, they took off zigzagging across the field, Hogan stumbling in his oversized fleece-lined boots that he had scrounged from an R.A.F. pilot in England. At the far side of the field they came to a short cliff above a dry creek bed. They slid down as far as they could, then jumped the last ten feet and hid beneath a rock overhang. They heard the sound of boots and German voices above them. It was all they could do to stifle their gasps for air. After a few minutes the Germans abandoned the chase.

Upon learning that Hogan was missing, Colonel Yeomans ordered his task force to resume its mission, which required clearing the roadblock outside of Maboge. By now it was reinforced by German troops, who held the superior position and denied further advance by Hogan's men. At 1100 hours, General Rose turned over operational command of the task force to Howze, who ordered them back to Hotton.

By 1630 the task force had reached Beffe, where it came

under heavy small arms and rocket fire from both sides of the road. One Sherman was knocked out. Unable to advance, the task force retreated in the direction from which they had just come, setting defensive positions on the outskirts of Marcouray.

Hogan's party, meanwhile, had spent the day dodging pockets of Germans. The entire area seemed saturated with enemy. Hogan paused at one point for a cigarette break. "You're sending smoke signals, Colonel," Worrell reminded him. They decided to split up to mitigate the risk of detection, and started for Hotton believing it was in American hands. Yet no matter which way they turned they kept encountering Germans. Cold and tired and hungry, Hogan kept imagining the Germans at the roadblock enjoying the Texas fruitcake he'd left in his jeep. Around midnight, he and his orderly and driver tried to get some sleep, the three of them curled up on the forest floor under Hogan's overcoat and a camouflage blanket of leaves.

The first German tank disabled on the morning of December 21st.

Oberleutnant Köhn's tank, knocked out in the orchard behind Soy Road.

80

Johannes Bayer and Gerhardt Tebbe

Lieutenant Edmund Socha

Corporal John Shields

Lieutenant Colonel Sam Hogan.

05

BY THE EARLY HOURS OF DECEMBER 22ND, IT WAS APPARENT to Rose that Alex Bolling would not be sending him anywhere near the level of help he had expected. Rose vented his frustration to General Ridgway, who assured him that he was working all the angles to reinforce him as soon as possible. Rose wasn't about to wait. At 0400 he summoned Bobby Howze to his new CP outside the village of Manhay. As usual, it was a short meeting. Rose's new plan to relieve the pressure on Hotton called for a two-pronged attack. The main thrust would come from Soy by a tank company under Captain Clifford Mize, less one platoon led by Lt. Smithers already there. At the same time, Task Force Hogan would fall back and attack toward Hotton from the southeast. It was wishful thinking at best that Hogan would be of any use. Not only was he missing, but his task force had been stopped by the enemy to his front, near Maboge, and had barely escaped the ambush outside of Beffe. Jump off for the attack was set for 0900. Fickessen learned of the plan at 0510.

"Hold Hotton at all cost," said Howze. "Utilize any available personnel as infantry . . . . Have tank-infantry task force [Warden] provide maximum support consistent with holding Hotton. Action must be aggressive."

Critical as the situation was in Hotton — and Ridgway certainly recognized it as such — it was but one of many flash spots on his radar screen. His phones and radios were swamped with calls for help, each more urgent than the one before. Ridgway's 18th Airborne Corps comprised the 82nd and 101st Airborne Divisions — the latter now surrounded at Bastogne — and was the main reserve force for all Allied Expeditionary Forces in Europe. His job was to parcel out the troops under his command wherever they were most needed to block the enemy's ever-deepening penetration into Belgium. He had promised Rose that help was on the way, and he intended to deliver.

Sometime after midnight the commanding officer and battalion heads of the 517th Parachute Regimental Combat Team arrived at Ridgway's headquarters. The 517th had been through two tough battle campaigns, first in Italy and then in the Champagne region of France, where it had sustained heavy losses. For the past couple weeks the 517th had been in Soissons, France, absorbing some 500 troop replacements, reconditioning equipment, and training for what everyone believed would be one last jump deep inside Germany come spring. Ridgway began his briefing by saying that the commanding officer of the first battalion to arrive there would report immediately to General Rose in Manhay. Lieutenant Colonel Bill Boyle knew that the legendary Ridgway was speaking to him. Boyle was out the door the moment Ridgway finished his briefing.

It was indicative of the widespread confusion that no one at Corps Headquarters could tell Boyle how to get to Manhay, nor were they able to provide him with a map or guide. When the MP directing traffic outside also was of no help, he flagged down a truck driver for directions. By 0600 he was standing in front of Rose.

"Rose was calm and cool," Boyle recalled, which impressed him considering that the picture painted by Ridgway "was not one to induce calm." The meeting lasted half an hour. Rose told Boyle that his 1st Battalion was now attached to Howze's Combat Command Reserve in Soy. Boyle arrived at Howze's CP at 0730 hours.

Tall and broad-shouldered with a sagging broom mustache, the Brooklyn-born Boyle looked more like a longshoreman stirred from a bad sleep than the West Pointer he was. The 27-year old paratrooper had graduated in the same class as Harvey Fraser, where they had run track and cross-country together. Nicknamed "Wild Bill" by his men for his strict work ethic and readiness to drop rank with anyone who challenged his leadership, Boyle had little use for spit-and-polish discipline. His drumbeat was all about combat reliability, which he understood was the product of rigorous training and mental toughness. In seven months of war he had asked nothing of his men that he wasn't prepared to do himself. "Colonel Boyle walked ahead of me a lot of times, and I was the first scout," one soldier remembered. "That was the kind of guy he was. Brave, very brave." Howze intended to put the scruffy officer and his battle-hardened troops to work the moment they arrived.

While they were sizing each other up, Jack Fickessen was butting heads with a Lt. Colonel from the 84th, demanding that he deploy his two-dozen troops on the north bank of the village. The light colonel reminded the abrasive Texan and junior officer that General Bolling's orders expressly forbade him from crossing the river. On this point there was nothing to discuss. He had, however, brought along a mortar crew, which he positioned behind the church. This gave McDonald two 81-mm mortars to work with. In addition, Bolling was sending them a platoon of tank destroyers, which he expected shortly.

John Anderson, meanwhile, was exchanging small talk with Chaplain Kraka and slowly acclimating to the sporatic pounding of artillery and mortar on the village. Since midnight he had sent two messages to Howze reporting "heavy stuff passing overhead," but had asked only once when help would arrive. Anderson had known Kraka since the summer of '42 while training in the Mohave desert, yet two years later he was still unsure what to make of the tobacco-chewing, whiskey-drinking priest with the pug face, especially now as he studied the pistol plainly visible outside Kraka's jacket. It puzzled him that a priest whose job it was to save souls could be so prepared to kill. Kraka was similarly perplexed by Anderson, albeit for less weighty philosophical reasons. For him, it all came down to Anderson's apparent indifference to baseball. In Kraka's mind this was almost un-American, a sin just barely offset by the Southerner's unshakeable faith in the Almighty. As they were talking, Phil Zulli hobbled downstairs toward the door. Anderson asked where he was going. Zulli said he was heading to his half-track for cigarettes.

"Be quick, it's hot out there," said Anderson.

Kraka walked outside with his friend, where Zulli paused.

"Father, I hope we'll be able to have Mass on Christmas Day. We should all be grateful to God for being with us during this crisis."

No sooner had the words left Zulli's lips when they heard the high-pitched whistle of an incoming shell. Kraka dove for the doorway as Zulli darted for his half-track. The shell landed in the street. When he looked up, Kraka saw Zulli lying face down and rushed to his side. At first he saw no sign of a wound, and thought he had been knocked unconscious by the shell's concussion. But the body was limp. On closer inspection, he spotted a thin trickle of blood oozing from a quarter-inch gash where a sliver of shell fragment had entered the back of Zulli's head.

When the body was carried inside the house and laid on table, all the color left Anderson's face. Time stopped as he watched Kraka administer the Sacrament of Extreme Unction, the two of them the last people to see him alive, to speak with him, perhaps his closest friends. Anderson crossed the room and stared from a window. It would be hours before Howze next heard from him.

* * *

AT 0835, A SIGNAL COMPANY OUTPOST PHONED FICKESSEN to say an enemy patrol was moving down Soy Road below the cemetery. Fickessen radioed Jack Warden to check it out. He reported back ten minutes later that he didn't see any infantry, but a single tank was approaching the village along the railroad track. The same outpost reported that the enemy patrol was entering the orchard. McDonald and Rodman saw the patrol from the schoolhouse. McDonald called to his mortar crew as Rodman rushed downstairs, where he paused briefly to phone Fickessen.

"Fire adjusted on enemy in orchard. One half-track and six infantry. Will report results."

It was a pattern begun the night before, with McDonald

directing mortar fire and the boyishly intense Rodman sprinting outside to spot the rounds and confirm damage. Suddenly Fickessen was getting calls from everyone.

"Quite a few men ran into woods below cemetery," said McDonald.

"Half-track and men with white flags coming west," said another voice.

"Germans in building to northeast wanting to surrender," said McDonald. Fickessen relayed the message to Warden. "Germans in northeast trying to give up. Hold fire and let them come in. Watch them."

"Tank on north side of building P375881," said Rodman, identifying the building by its map-grid coordinates. This was the tank Warden had seen on the railroad track. Now it was in the orchard behind an apple tree. From across the river, Lieutenant Charlie Bryson saw it, too.

Bryson had just arrived from Marche with four M18 tank destroyers, grudgingly sent there by General Bolling who wasn't convinced the situation in Hotton was serious but was being worn down by the repeated calls for help. The M18 — popularly known as the *Hellcat* — was built to chase tanks. Smaller than the Sherman and half the weight, the Hellcat was the fastest and most maneuverable tracked vehicle then in use by the Army. It had an open 360-degree traverse turret and a 76-mm high-velocity gun. Its vulnerability was its thin armor, only an inch and a half at its thickest point. From a pure killing standpoint, however, it was equal to the German Panther.

Three of Bryson's Hellcats had a clear shot at the Panther, which meant the Panther also had a clear shot at them. They fired seven rounds in a series of three, then two, then two more, retiring after each volley behind some buildings along Marche Road. At least two of the rounds scored hits but failed to kill the Panther; the other rounds chewed up the orchard, reducing the apple tree to wood chips. The Panther replied with five rounds, all off target, but sufficient to drive the tank destroyers into hiding long enough for the Panther to retreat to the woods. Although ineffective, Bryson's firing provided a much needed morale boost to the Americans across the river, most of whom could not see the Hellcats and assumed that friendly artillery had done the job.

The reorganized troops in Hotton were having a far better morning than the two forces charged with rescuing them. At 1035 Howze informed Rose that Captain Mize had met strong anti-tank and small arms fire from *Quatre Bras* and had lost one tank. By 1225, Mize had lost seven of his fifteen tanks, five Shermans and two Stuarts. Task Force Hogan was doing no better. At 1140, again outside of Beffe, they reported taking heavy fire to their front while fighting off enemy patrols to their rear. Half an hour later they requested air support, only to be told that planes were grounded due to poor visibility. At 1340, they reported that a full battalion of German infantry occupied the village and they were pulling back to Marcouray to "get good defending." The only good news was that Sam Hogan had surfaced, literally stumbling from the woods into the path of his retreating task force.

Part of the reason the troops in Hotton were doing as well as they were was because Johannes Bayer had pulled most of his tanks from the village to fend off the attack from Soy. That accomplished, five German tanks now appeared below the cemetery determined to break through. Two Panthers moved in behind the Verdin farmhouse on the east side of the connector road.

Mike McDonald had been watching Germans running to and from the Verdin house all day, peppering them with mortar. Three grenadiers had been shot while firing from behind a large mill stone near the house. Chaplain Kraka, acting as interpreter in the interrogation of a prisoner, had learned that the house was the enemy's forward command post. McDonald had refrained from targeting the house after observing an old man, obviously a civilian, helping to carry the enemy wounded inside. He assumed there were other civilians in the house.

Across the river, Charlie Bryson knew nothing of this. He was just looking for something to shoot at when he spotted one of the tanks. A little before 1500, he fired two rounds, missing the Panther but gutting the house. The tank moved to the back of the house out of Bryson's field of vision. He fired a third round in an attempt to flush it out, further crumpling the stone building. A squad from Fickessen's engineers had been watching the action from the bluff above LaRoche Road. Realizing the tank destroyers could do much better firing from their position, they sent a runner to bring them up. When they arrived nearly an hour later, Bryson broke into a big toothy grin. The location offered a clear field of fire to the northeast and excellent range, around 500 yards to the Verdin house. Moreover, he now could see five tanks, one half-track and an ammo carrier dispersed across the eastern edge of the village. The former insurance agent practically giggled with glee.

While Bryson formulated a firing plan, 70-year-old Herbert Verdin — the civilian McDonald had seen hauling the wounded Germans — was cowering with his wife and daughter in the cellar of their demolished home. Part of the second floor had collapsed on top of the cellar door, filling the dank space with dust and smoke. The daughter knew that her husband and children, hiding in the nearby Evrard farmhouse, had seen her parents' home destroyed and probably feared they were dead. Scratching the words "We are all safe" on a piece of paper, she crawled from the cellar to plead with a grenadier to take the message to her family. Remarkably, he agreed to do so, dashing under fire from the schoolhouse. "You must leave here," he told the husband after delivering the message. "Your house will be destroyed." The husband insisted on returning with him to bring back his wife and family. After much wrangling, the soldier acquiesced. The two of them ran back to the Verdin house. "Now go," said the soldier, shooing the four Belgians from the house. Another grenadier, however, thought the civilians might be of value and started after them. Exiting the house, he was about to overtake them when he plunged waist deep into the Verdin cesspool uncovered by one of McDonald's mortars. The story of the first grenadier's humanity and courage in carrying the daughter's message, followed by the second German's swim in the cesspool, would spread among *les Hottonais* in the days to come. It's doubtful anyone processed these conflicting acts of mercy and cruelty beyond wishing that more Germans had fallen into the Verdin sewer.

Charlie Bryson and his Hellcat commanders were lying on their stomachs at the edge of the bluff, picking their targets.

Bryson decided to position three of his tank destroyers on a line 50 yards apart and 25 yards back from the edge of the bluff, and ordered gun tubes turned around to fire over their rear. On his signal, the tank destroyers would back up to the bluff's edge and fire simultaneously on the most vulnerable Panther, then each would fire on a second tank before driving forward to escape returning fire. Radios were turned on and the commanders reported to Bryson. They set their watches for two minutes.

Below them, in the Lobet beer parlor on LaRoche Road, an officer from the 84th was aware of what Bryson was up to and invited several civilians to join him at the window for the fireworks. Two minutes passed. All at once the village was filled with thunder and a series of explosions. The first of Bryson's targets took three direct hits to its side and burst into flames, its four-man crew instantly cremated. A second tank was hit, exploding its ammunition bin and setting a nearby haystack in flames. Two rounds bounced off a third tank before it also exploded, the blast later attributed to land mines stacked behind the turret.

"The plan worked out very well," Bryson recalled in his after-action report. "It seemed that all hell broke loose, and to see three guns slamming away at once and see the results, a mass of wreckage and flaming tanks, and have it all happen so quickly and smoothly was a wonderful sight." Bryson felt no remorse over the men they had killed, only satisfaction that their actions had saved American lives, including his own.

It wasn't a wonderful sight for Johannes Bayer, watching from the woods as his tanks burned and infantry retreated. The Americans were much stronger than he had supposed. Between the mortar and machine gun fire, and now these big guns, he had been unable to reinforce his troops holed up in the houses on Soy Road, much less seize the bridge that would allow him to keep moving toward the Meuse. They were losing the initiative. Daylight was killing them. They would have to attack at night. However, Bayer had just gotten word that the main bridge in LaRoche was intact and undefended, presenting him with another way over the Ourthe. Rather than squander precious time and resources in Hotton, the decision was made to pull the 116th back to LaRoche, cross the river there and push west through the corridor between Marche and Hotton. Bayer's orders were to stay put until relieved by elements of the 560th *Volksgrenadiers* Division – specifically, the 1129th Regiment – which would protect his rear flank. It was a scenario General Ridgway had anticipated, and the reason Bolling had stubbornly refused to commit his forces to the fight in Hotton. In the meantime, Bayer readied his troops for a final attack.

* * *

Bill Boyle's 1st Battalion detrucked in the woods above Soy about the time Charlie Bryson was shooting up the Verdin house. They had been sitting in open trucks for 21 hours, lamenting their lack of winter clothing while pondering what lay ahead. Seven truckloads of paratroopers, representing a quarter of Boyle's battalion, had gotten lost en route in the impenetrable fog and freezing drizzle. There was no time to wait for them or to go looking for them. Boyle had his men stack bedrolls, collect ammo and prepare to move out. Howze radioed for a status report at 1630.

"Can you jump off at 1700?"

"No," said Boyle.

"1730?"

"I could."

"It will be dark then," said Howze. "Can you make it 1700?"

"Well, yes."

"Okay, I'll give you back five minutes then. Jump off at 1705."

Howze's rush to get them moving was partly due to the latest message from Sam Hogan. Now in Marcouray, Hogan's vehicles were running out of gas, which meant they would be stuck there unless resupplied. This was a long shot given the nearest fuel dump was in Barvaux, 15 miles away, and any resupply would have to go through Soy, beyond which the area was teeming with enemy. Howze told Hogan they were working the problem. Hogan correctly understood this to mean the chances of reaching him were slim. He coolly radioed back that he had plenty of ammo and food, adding that the artillery was "going both ways." Howze now knew that Hogan would be of no help clearing up the Hotton situation, and moreover, that he had just become a situation himself. He needed Boyle's paratroopers more than ever.

The terrain below Soy was a vast, gently sloping field framed by Soy Road to the east and the railroad line from Hotton to the west, a quarter-mile wide and nearly a mile to the *Sur les Hys* woods and the *Quatre Bras* road junction. Johannes Bayer's forces were dug-in just back from the tree line between

Quatre Bras and the railroad line. Two *Jagdpanser IV* tank destroyers flanked either side of *Quatre Bras*, joined by at least one *SdKfz 251/9* half-track with a 75-mm tank gun. Like the American Hellcat, the *Jagdpanser IV* was lighter and faster than its bigger cousins but every bit as dangerous to American armor, especially the thin-skinned Stuarts. Lacking turrets, their powerful guns were mounted in the front hull giving them a low silhouette that made them harder to hit, particularly when dug-in as they were here. The trade-off was mobility, which left them vulnerable to rocket attack if enemy infantry evaded their twin front-firing machine guns. In addition to these tank killers, there were a large but unknown number of grenadiers hunkered down in some forty slit trenches facing out over the field, many of them fortified with *MG 42s*. Arguably the finest machine gun used in WWII, the *MG 42* was theoretically capable of firing more than 1,500 rounds per minute, a cyclic rate so intense it sounded to some like linoleum tearing. As always, the challenge confronting an attacking force was just getting close enough to return fire effectively. Boyle's paratroopers had to move almost a mile over largely open field.

The 517th — about 450 men — lumbered past Howze's CP a little before 1800. Just below the village, they dispersed into a narrow section of field east of Soy Road. Under a thin veil of moonlight, they saw the American tanks knocked out earlier in the day, some still burning, others appearing as dark angular shadows on the barren ground. Boyle's paratroopers advanced about 350 yards when they came under fire. Howze heard the clatter and boom from his CP as he left to confer again with Rose. A moment before, he had received a message from Anderson that Hotton was under attack by tanks and infantry. "Need help," Anderson pleaded.

* * *

Mike McDonald had been standing at his school-house observation post for 26 hours. He had exhausted his entire stockpile of flares fed by the mortar crew positioned behind the *Fanfare Royale* theatre, and his phone line to the 84th's mortar squad behind the church across the river had been cut by enemy shell fire. At 1835, he phoned Fickessen to relay his fire mission.

"Enemy tanks and infantry in vicinity of P373886. Request to 334th to put flares out there."

For Fickessen, there was no question a new attack was underway. Jack Warden also reported tanks moving in, and Rodman was taking small arms fire, which meant German infantry had infiltrated the area around the schoolhouse. At 1903, Anderson sent out another SOS. "Being attacked, need help desperately."

At the prayer chapel marking the northern entrance to the village, the men under Paul Copeland were shooting into the darkness at everything and nothing. Fence posts had been chewed up, and a prized Belgian steer decapitated by a .50 caliber machine gun when it ambled into their field of fire. Until that morning, Copeland had been recreation officer Phil Zulli's administrative assistant, a perfect job-fit for the bullshitting sergeant. Even Anderson was amused by Copeland's bottomless well of one-liners — "So whatuya think, is sex here to stay?"

Yet the sergeant was holding up remarkably well in his first exposure to combat. More cheerleader than captain, he cajoled the men into firing their weapons by reminding them "You can't kill 'em if you don't shoot 'em." Earlier in the afternoon he had to order one of them, a cook, to turn over his machine gun after noticing that he had been shot in the neck. Now the field to the east lit up under McDonald's flares. Copeland's men saw two columns of about 70 grenadiers advancing toward them and let loose with everything they had. McDonald adjusted mortar fire from the schoolhouse.

"Firing north on attacking enemy," he told Fickessen. "Many enemy believed wounded."

At the sawmill, situated between the schoolhouse and Copeland's position, Rodman's ad hoc platoon was looking out at yet more enemy infantry coming toward them. The entire field between the connector road and the railroad embankment was swarming with Germans.

"Firing concentration on P374882," McDonald notified Fickessen. It would be his last call of the night.

Bayer's scouts had been looking for his observation post all day, searching every high window for the slightest shadow or movement. Assuming they were being watched from the schoolhouse, they had targeted the building with artillery and mortar. Wrecked upturned vehicles were on every side. At 2040 hours, Rodman reported that the enemy was "closing in around my position." As that message went out, a *Panzerfaust* rocket slammed into the window casement where McDonald was standing, showering him with brick and glass and hurling him across the room. Rodman rushed upstairs to check on him as Chaplain Kraka and another man were carrying him down. Rodman remained on the second floor only a minute when a second rocket sailed through the same window striking a ceiling beam, collapsing a section of attic that caused the floor under him to crash into the kitchen below. A medic pulled him from the heap of beams and flooring. "I'm okay, I'm okay," said Rodman, looking around for his rifle and helmet. In fact, he had just fractured two vertebrae and part of his sacrum.

All of the Americans north of the schoolhouse now abandoned their positions, swinging back like a screen door toward Melreux Road. Copeland led his men, including two wounded, on a mile-long trek to the west, then south to the river and across the bridge to Fickessen's CP. The troops at the sawmill joined others fleeing the schoolhouse to form a defensive line along the railroad embankment and extending west past Anderson's CP. The northeast quadrant of the village was now in enemy hands, along with two-thirds of the houses on Soy Road. Around 2200 the attack suddenly stopped, bewildering the Americans. Unbeknownst to them, Johannes Bayer's men had been relieved by elements of the 560th Volkgrenadiers under the command of *Oberstleutnant* Helmut Zander. *Kampfgruppe* Bayer set out for the Ourthe River crossing in LaRoche.

"That was the worst fight I got into the whole damn war," Rodman recalled. "The thing was on. The show was going and everyone for themselves. These guys were fighting like hell." In almost the same breath, he described watching a priest walk along the railroad enbankment conferring his blessing of Absolution on the Americans, oblivious to the sporadic shell and rifle fire around him. "It seemed like he was out there for hours, going from one foxhole to another. It was the bravest goddamn thing I ever saw. I thought he was a saint."

Later that night Fickessen summarized the four-hour battle. "Enemy infantry attack beginning 1800 stopped 2200. Holding line 372879 to 372883 to 365883 with covering fire to the north from 84th Div. arty." He estimated the day's casualties at three killed and ten wounded. If accurate, it brought the total number of dead, wounded and missing since the previous morning to forty-eight. His figures did not include Lt. Socha's losses in Melines, or those of Captain Mize in the field below Soy.

* * *

BILL BOYLE WAS MAKING NO HEADWAY in his attack. At 2110, he radioed Howze that he was taking fire from two sides. This wasn't the result Howze had hoped for. He reminded Boyle that it was "imperative" to push the attack and "reach Hotton as quickly as possible."

There weren't many options open to Boyle given the terrain. There was simply too much firepower to his front — machine gun, mortar and tank fire — and too little cover. He decided to split his forces to try to flank the German position, sending two platoons into the sloping woods toward Melines, where they would then advance uphill to *Quatre Bras*. It wasn't long before the flanking force came under fire, the ink-black woods lighting up with tracer rounds. Here at least there was plenty of cover. Spreading out, the paratroopers worked their way toward the fire, silencing two machine guns with grenades.

Immediately they heard the distinctive creak and rattle of tracked vehicles. The platoons divided, moving on either side of the road that Socha's patrol had taken the previous morning. Soon they could make out two light armored personnel carriers guarded by grenadiers. The platoon positioned below the road targeted the lead half-track while the other closed on the second. Clark Archer recalled that the grenadiers were "eliminated relatively quickly." At least one of the half-tracks was taken out by bazooka.

The firing had not gone unnoticed. Now the paratroopers heard what sounded like tanks heading their way. Deciding their flanking mission was unfeasible, they rejoined the main force. Howze had just returned from another meeting with General Rose. He summoned Boyle to his CP.

"The Commanding General insists that this is to be cleared up tonight if humanly possible," he told Boyle. "This is the most important operation in the Allied Expeditionary Forces. We have got to do it. We must fight night and day to do it." If that wasn't clear enough, Howze double-stamped the message: "Shove this attack through tonight."

Boyle had come to fight, but he wasn't about to sacrifice his men on a whim, particularly for some colonel he had just met. He intended to protect his men as best he could so they at least had a fighting chance. Right now, he told Howze, crossing that field was a mistake. Howze couldn't disagree since he had left seven tanks on the same field earlier that day, while inflicting little or no damage on the enemy. Together they hatched a new plan. If the road to Ny was open, as they believed it was, then Boyle would take one company through Ny to Barvaux

Road, then south to Hotton. It was the same route the Warden-Smithers task force had taken the morning before. Once there, they would sweep the enemy from the village and attack east toward Soy. The rest of the 517th, under the command of Major Don Fraser, would attack toward Hotton. When the two forces joined up, they would have purged the enemy from the *Sur les Hys* woods and secured the three-mile line between the two villages.

They spent an hour and a half sorting out the details. Howze reported the plan to Rose, who replied by sending him two platoons of about 60 men from the 509th Parachute Infantry Regiment, courtesy of Matt Ridgway. They would be folded into Don Fraser's force attacking from Soy. The clock showed it was now December 23rd. It was the beginning of what would be a very bloody day.

The Hotton cemetery abutting Soy Road.

The back of the schoolhouse and location of Lt. McDonald's observation post damaged by a *Panzerfaust* rocket.

McDonald's view to the east toward the *Sur les Hys* woods.

Destroyed German tanks and vehicles behind the Verdin house,
and Lieutenant Charlie Bryson *(inset)*.

Chapelle Notre-Dame de Consolation where the troops under
Sergeant Paul Copeland were deployed.

06.

WITH THE LOSS OF THE NORTHEAST QUADRANT OF THE VIL-
lage, Fickessen pulled the squad from the observation post above
LaRoche Road and sent them to reinforce Rodman's men along
the railroad line. German shells continued to sprinkle in and
occasional rifle fire was exchanged in the orchard. The muffled
moans of enemy wounded wafted from the home of Dr. Du-
chateau, who had exhausted his medicinal supplies treating the
bloodied troops, ripping his own bed sheets for bandages. At
0300 hours, John Anderson radioed Howze that all was calm.
He had not heard the blast minutes earlier from a Panzerfaust
rocket tearing into one of Lieutenant Smither's tanks below
the railroad embankment, nor had he heard the ensuing fire as
Warden's riflemen picked off the Panzerfaust team hovering
nearby. Warden pulled five men from the tank, two of whom
would die from their wounds. At 0400, having had no success
dislodging the enemy from the houses along Soy Road, Warden
ordered his men to fall back toward the bridge in advance of
calling in artillery from the 84th.

At 0455, Anderson radioed the news Howze had been
waiting for: "Friendly tanks and infantry entering town from
north." Boyle's force had arrived. It had taken his hundred or
so paratroopers an hour and a half riding in half-tracks to cover
the three miles from Soy. "They made a helluva racket coming
into town," one officer remembered. "It must have scared the
Krauts into leaving because there was no more action around

the schoolhouse after they came in. After that, all the fighting was down by the river."

Rodman met Boyle on the street near the schoolhouse. He briefed him on the situation then pointed out, from the railroad embankment, the houses along Soy Road where the enemy could be found. They quickly agreed the 3rd Armored troops would defend Boyle's northern flank while he flushed them out. Boyle crossed the bridge to meet with Fickessen, parking his men in the steepleless church so they could catch a few hours of much needed sleep. The lieutenant colonel in command of the 20-odd troops from the 84th was in Fickessen's CP. He explained for the umpteenth time that his orders forbade him from deploying his men on the other side of the river. Boyle hadn't asked for help; he just wanted to know who was where. At 0715, Fickessen radioed Howze that Boyle's men "were preparing to continue on their mission." Howze forwarded the news to General Rose.

Although Germans occupied two-thirds of the houses on Soy Road, the acute danger of losing Hotton had passed. Indeed, Bobby Howze fully expected Boyle's men to clear the enemy from the village by noon and link up with Don Fraser's force attacking from Soy by nightfall. It's unclear why he believed this timetable was achievable given the situation at *Quatre Bras*, where Bayer's forces had repulsed two major attacks and the enemy remained firmly entrenched. It was as though the mere act of ordering it to happen spelled success.

* * *

IN THE HILLTOP VILLAGE OF MARCOURAY, SAM HOGAN HAD enjoyed a largely uneventful night, interrupted briefly when his tankers took target practice on some enemy vehicles across the river. "We had a regular turkey shoot," Hogan later wrote, recalling how Germans kept returning to a jeep to retrieve something of value. "Every time they would approach it we would lay in a round of tank fire," until eventually there was nothing left of the jeep or its contents to retrieve. At 0100 hours on the December 23rd, Howze radioed that help was on the way.

"Attacking now to clear Soy-Hotton area. When this completed we attack toward you. Have sent your request for medical supplies forward and expect you to get them tomorrow."

Howze was exhausted: tomorrow meant today. Hogan, however, wasn't kidding himself that help would be coming anytime soon. Hotton was eight miles away, and as best he could tell the entire area in between was in enemy hands. He knew that Howze would do everything in his power to reach him. If he was alarmed by his situation he didn't show it. He replied that he still had some gas — despite an earlier report to the contrary — and plenty of ammo to throw back at the enemy.

At 0725, Hogan reported no contact with the enemy but noted considerable movement in the area. He had set roadblocks on the main road leading in and out of the village, each comprised of an M3 Sherman and a reconnaissance platoon. An hour later two armored cars each carrying about twenty Germans approached the eastern roadblock, apparently catching his men dozing. The first car made it through and sped west through the village, the second car forced to retreat under fire from the reconnaissance troopers. Hogan had just stepped outside his command post when the first car passed him. It was, he later wrote, "a shattering experience before breakfast." He alerted his men at the western roadblock, then radioed to the tank commander at the other demanding to know how the car had gotten through. The tanker stuttered the excuse that condensation in the gun turret had frozen overnight, preventing him from swinging the gun at the enemy car. Hogan knew he had fallen asleep. "It's a wonder my language didn't thaw his turret ring," said Hogan. He reported the incident to Howze at 1025.

"Two enemy armored cars and three-zero men tried to come in. We knocked out one car, took 5 PWs [prisoners] and killed several. Beating bushes for more. Some have US uniforms, one had Red Cross band and under arms. Shall we conduct court proceedings?"

Hogan's reference to "court proceedings" was code for permission to execute the prisoners. Combatants disguised in the uniform of their enemy, especially medics and clergy, were considered spies and therefore outside the protections of the Geneva Convention. Spies were executed. By some accounts, this had been the fate of the twenty-one "civilians" captured by Harvey Fraser's engineers three days earlier. Howze replied at 1315.

"Answer to your message of 1025 is 'Yes.'"

In his later account of the episode, Hogan neglected to mention that the prisoners were dressed as GIs, describing the scene quite differently. "Four of five Germans were lying head to foot in the ditch along side of the road. Before anyone could stop him, a lieutenant from the Reconnaissance Company had pulled his .45 and shot two of them in the back of the head. As he was standing over the third German prior to shooting, the second one, who had only been creased, got up. The lieutenant was disarmed and the remaining Germans made prisoners."

Dead or alive, prisoners were the least of Hogan's concerns. He needed medical supplies and blood for his wounded — specifically, "type O whole blood, 500cc to 1000" — and he needed it soon. The weather had cleared allowing supplies to be dropped by air. Howze instructed him to form a circle of vehicles, 60 feet in diameter, marked with display panels to identify their position.

At 1400 Hogan got word that an enemy vehicle flying a white flag had been stopped at the western roadblock. Three Germans were in the car, two officers and an interpreter. Hogan ordered them blindfolded and led in circles to his CP. When they were delivered he was handed a note stating that his task force was surrounded. Hogan had questions, but when it turned out the interpreter could barely speak English, he summoned his Yiddish-speaking battalion surgeon to fill the role. After much back and forth it was decided that they were there to solicit his surrender, and, as a demonstration of good faith, to invite one of Hogan's officers to tour the German positions to confirm the hopelessness of their situation. Tempted as he was to collect this valuable intelligence, Hogan knew that whomever he sent would not be coming back. "If you want this town come right in and take it," he told the envoys before releasing them. He radioed Howze at 1445.

"Just had party come in to request surrender. They entered on main road from Beffe. They are from a General, Div. Comdr. They state we are surrounded by 3 Panzer Divs. We turned it down."

Hogan didn't doubt that he was surrounded, but three Panzer divisions added up to 30,000 men at full strength. He held the high ground, but evidently the Germans didn't realize how small his task force was. Not that it mattered. The very notion of surrender was anathema to him and ran counter to everything he had been trained to do as a soldier. The objective in war was to inflict maximum damage on one's enemy at a minimum cost, and then move on to fight another day. He still had plenty of firepower and his casualties had been light – one dead and a dozen wounded. Hogan had no intention of giving up.

He spent the rest of the afternoon waiting for supplies. Howze told him the drop would be made at 1300, and instructed Hogan to put out cerise panels in the shape of a large T to mark the drop zone. He was still waiting for the drop at 1825 when he radioed Howze: "Is the situation so bad you can't send it to us?" In fact, the promised supply mission had come through right on schedule when it was hit by anti-aircraft fire. Hogan's men saw two C-47s go down and watched the airmen bail out, several hitting trees before their chutes could deploy. Remarkably, no one had bothered to tell Hogan.

* * *

THE COORDINATED ATTACKS BY THE 517TH GOT OFF TO A slow start. Boyle had radio problems, and it was nearly 1100 before Howze learned of the stiff resistance he was encountering on Soy Road. Fifteen minutes later, Boyle reported that it would take another hour to clear the village.

"Expedite," said Howze.

"Will take another hour," Boyle answered.

Rodman, meanwhile, had returned to the schoolhouse and redeployed his men to the positions they had given up the night before. There was no sign of the enemy north of the railroad embankment. McDonald was back, too, bruised and bandaged and still cured of his pneumonia. Fickessen phoned him to lay down fire on an enemy mortar position at the eastern edge of the village. Howze radioed Boyle at 1240.

"Give me the situation there now."

"We have just started to attack."

"Keep them going as fast as you can. Keep that radio with you as close as possible."

Don Fraser was having no better success getting across the field below Soy. At five-foot-eight and 135 pounds, the 26-year old major and former mail clerk was a scaled-down copy of his boss. Nicknamed "Iron Duke," Fraser had earned a Silver Star two months earlier for carrying two wounded paratroopers to safety while under 20-millimeter cannon fire. When later asked to assess Fraser's qualities as a soldier, Boyle replied in typically terse fashion: "Let me put it this way. He came to me out of jump school as a second lieutenant, and I recommended him for promotion three times." If ever two men were cut from the same cloth, these were the two.

Helmut Zander's 1129th Regiment had taken over the positions previously held by *Kampfgruppe* Bayer. The plan called for Fraser's force, accompanied by ten tanks under the command of Captain Mize, to attack toward Melines – designated "Place A" – then uphill to *Quatre Bras* and the *Sur les Hys* woods. At 0850, Fraser called in artillery – 75-mm guns and 105-mm howitzers – in preparation for the attack. The effectiveness of the bombardment, however, was lost when Mize's tankers weren't ready to jump off. At 0955, Howze reported to an increasingly impatient Rose. "Force of 3 platoons infantry with 5 medium and 5 light tanks have attacked." Mize radioed at noon.

"We are nearly at Place A and are in firefight. Resistance is not too heavy. Incoming mail is rather heavy."

"Are the others moving along?" said Howze, referring to Fraser's men.

"As well as they can."

But it was clear to both Mize and Fraser that they were bogged down. Fraser requested permission to quit the attack in favor of moving to Hotton, via Ny, to consolidate his forces with Boyle's.

"Permission refused," Howze answered. "Work down left of [Soy] road to clear out and join your commanding officer from that direction."

The 517th had tried exactly that the night before and had gotten nowhere. "Colonel, you're sending us to the boneyard," said Fraser.

It now clicked with Howze that a frontal attack in this terrain was futile. He ordered the task force back to Soy. Once there it was organized into two columns and ordered to move along the railroad line on the western rim of the field below Soy, then attack through the *Sur le Hys* woods above Ny. The downside of the new plan – soon to be a reality – was that the task force would be vulnerable to the German armor until it reached the edge of the woods. At 1438, Mize reported that he had only three useable tanks left. Two minutes later, Fraser reported 40 casualties. Dean Robbins, commanding officer of B Company, called for his lead scout.

"Get into those woods and tell me what's there."

Private First Class Melvin Biddle had been working in an Indiana grocery store when he was drafted two years earlier. Five-foot-ten and country handsome, the 21 year-old Biddle looked like a poster boy for paratroopers. Armed with a .30 caliber M-1 rifle, grenades and a knife, he set out alone through the thick underbrush along the railroad line, moving in short dashes until he had crossed the road from Ny to *Quatre Bras* and was well into the woods. So dense were the trees that his visibility was less than thirty yards in daylight. He spotted three Germans in a slit trench near the railroad track. They didn't see him. Crouching beside a tree, he took aim at the helmet of the nearest German. "I felt bad about shooting him because he was an older guy, maybe forty," Biddle remembered. For an instant he considered taking the other two as prisoners but changed his mind when they raised their rifles. He shot a second German in the gut, the third ran. Biddle fired twice, both rounds striking him between the shoulder blades but failing to knock him down. He approached the second soldier, who was on his back clutching his stomach, gazing plaintively at Biddle. "He looked just like me, blond and blue-eyed. He was awfully hard hit. I knew he didn't have long." The paratrooper reached down and loosened the dying soldier's belt.

The woods around him now exploded from friendly fire, causing Biddle to hug the ground, then stopped as abruptly as it began. He moved in a diagonal path in the direction of Soy

Road. Up ahead he saw several vehicles with white stars painted on the doors, clearly American. Creeping forward he heard German voices. Deciding to report what he'd seen, he squirreled his way back through the woods to the rest of his company. Captain Robbins heard him out, then told him to return and snatch a prisoner for interrogation. Robbins assigned two men to accompany Biddle on the mission.

As Biddle's team set out, Boyle reported that he was "meeting strong counterattack" but had cleared three-quarters of the houses along Soy Road. At 1550 hours, Maurice Rose arrived unannounced at Howze's CP. He was, to put it mildly, displeased by Boyle's lack of progress and with Howze in general.

"The town must be definitely held . . . Are they still pushing?"

"Yes, they're pushing," said Howze.

"Have you got air [support]?

"No."

"Did you know that air was available?"

"No."

The famously unemotional Rose blanched. For the first time in a week, the skies had cleared enough that American planes could fly, which meant commanders on the ground could get close-air support for their tankers and infantry. But requesting air support and getting it took time. It was too late to get it today.

"Clearing Hotton is the first priority," he told Howze. "Work this thing over first. Impress on every individual that we must stay right here or there will be a war to be fought all over again and we won't be here to fight it."

A mile away, Biddle's snatching party was crouched in the woods waiting for their prey. Nearly dusk, it looked like night under the dense canopy of trees. A German officer appeared from behind one of the American trucks. Although he was lead scout, Biddle deferred to the sergeant next to him to do something. Nothing happened. Biddle looked over at him. He saw the sergeant mouthing the words "Halt! Halt!", but the command was issued in such a low whisper that Biddle wondered if he had lost his voice. The officer had heard nothing. "Halt!" the sergeant whispered again, then fired two shots at the officer from a range of 15 yards, both missing. The officer wheeled in the direction of the *pop-pop* as the rounds snapped past him, fumbled for his pistol and began firing.

"I was so bum-fuzzled by this time I couldn't shoot him," said Biddle. "Next thing I knew we were all running."

Biddle was so confused he ran straight toward the enemy's forward positions facing out over the field, while the other two paratroopers sprinted for the railroad line, which ultimately led them back to their company. For the Indiana farm boy, it was the beginning of a long night spent mostly on his stomach, fighting the numbing cold while slowly inching his way from the woods.

At 1645, Fickessen called a meeting of all unit commanders, including Boyle, to organize a defense of the village. No adjustments were made: the paratroopers would defend to the east, everyone else to the north and west. Boyle checked in with Howze at 1710.

"The situation is we have one-half of this objective. Right in the heart of the objective they are receiving small arms fire –

some arty – there are some Jerries in there."

"Do you know the situation of your executive officer?" said Howze.

"I have the situation from him about an hour ago. His continued progress will aid me, but from my last message from him, he would be of no immediate help."

"That town must be held at all costs."

"It will be held."

"How much of it do you hold?"

"It will be held. We are not actually driven back. We made a partially inaccurate report before — approximately ¼ in direction you had intended to move. Further progress appears to be impossible at this time."

"I am going to continue pushing your Ex.O. Be prepared for him and see him if we can do anything."

By 1830, the forward elements of Fraser's force had penetrated the northern edge of the *Sur les Hys* woods. It had taken six hours and more than 50 casualties to get there. Among the first to reach the tree line was Lieutenant Harry Allingham, a platoon leader from C Company. Allingham was approaching the narrow road from Ny to *Quatre Bras* when he was sprayed by machine gun fire. Hit multiple times, he nevertheless managed to call for his runner to bring up the rest of his platoon. Moments later, Allingham was hit by another burst, killing him. One of the rounds nicked a white phosphorous grenade that he carried in a canteen cover on his belt, setting him aflame. A dozen or more paratroopers were cut down. Allingham's corpse would burn for hours, the stench of charred flesh filling the woods. This was the backdrop when Howze radioed Fraser at

1848.

"Do you control the road?"

"No, not as yet."

"Explain."

"We have not set any roadblock as yet."

"Could you set up a block at that point on Place A?"

"I do not believe I have enough for that."

"Maintain your present progress and attempt to secure the road behind you. I want you to maintain the line A-B on the road."

"I can try but the set-up is not favorable to me."

"You come back here and see me," said Howze.

Place A was the road junction in Melines, one arm of which curled uphill to *Quatre Bras*. From there it proceeded west past the dead Allingham before curving north and west to the village of Ny. Place B was just north of where the road curved toward Ny. Fraser arrived at Howze's CP an hour later.

"Where is Jerry?" said Howze.

"Every side of us but in back of us . . . hit small arms, machine gun and sniper fire. Very heavily wooded. They ran off in the woods, tanks shooting at us, we're getting shell fire."

"Tomorrow, you and your commanding officer are going to make contact. Your mission is to clear out the road in that area. We must clean up this road and save Hotton."

Fraser nodded. He knew what needed to be done and left to rejoin his men. At 2145 he reported that *Quatre Bras* had been taken.

"Hold that crossroads at all cost," said Howze.

Although Fraser had no way of knowing it, part of their

success was attributable to lost scout Melvin Biddle, still burrowed in the woods and trying to make his way out. Since fleeing the surreal scene at the American trucks hours earlier, he had stumbled upon three enemy machine gun nests, which he had taken out with a combination of grenade and rifle fire, killing at least five more Germans. Enemy patrols had combed the woods hunting him, at one point stepping on his hand as he lay motionless on the forest floor. He, too, had seen the bright light of Allingham's burning corpse, but could not have imagined what he was seeing. He also heard a plane pass overhead practically touching the treetops, followed by a burst of 20-mm cannon fire from a second plane. A moment later, the earth trembled as the first plane – a German *Junker Ju* 88 – crashed into the field near *Quatre Bras*. A pilot thrown from the plane lay crumpled on the ground, calling for his mother: "*Mutti, Mutti.*" Biddle heard several shots and the moaning stopped. "That oughta hold the bastard," someone said.

At 2213, Rose called Howze to find out whether Hogan had received his supplies. Howze said no.

"You report to this CP immediately," said Rose, his tone implying a trip to the woodshed.

A chastened Howze was back in Soy by 2310. He had not slept since the early morning of the 21st, nearly three days now, subsisting entirely on cigarettes and coffee. His mouth tasted like dirt. He radioed Hogan.

"Every effort being made to drop ammo, gas, rations and medical supplies. Time for tomorrow's mission later."

Lieutenant Colonel Bill Boyle *(left)* and Major Don Fraser.

PFC Melvin Biddle *(left)* and *Oberstleutnant* Helmut Zander.

07.

FRASER'S MEN SPENT THE EARLY HOURS OF DECEMBER 24TH tightening their grip on *Quatre Bras*. Tree bursts from artillery combined with machine gun fire denied them further penetration into the woods.

"Is everything okay?" Howze radioed Fraser.

"We are still working on it."

At 0200, General Rose sent a line officer to Howze's CP with instructions to suspend the paratrooper attacks until 0815. Rose had good reasons for doing this. He knew the 517th had suffered significant casualties, and recognized that they would have better success in daylight when they could actually see the enemy. He also had drummed up another 80 paratroopers from the 509th, which would take time to assimilate with Fraser's force. More reinforcements were due to arrive later in the day, though it's unclear whether Rose shared this news with Howze. By 0400, the firing around *Quatre Bras* had abated, allowing Fraser to evacuate his wounded. Melvin Biddle emerged from the woods.

His company commander, Dean Robbins, had assumed Biddle was dead when he failed to return with the other two scouts. No one imagined he could still be alive given the number of Germans in the woods and the intensity of fire going both ways. Biddle described what he had seen during his 15 hours of skulking in the forest, noting the position of enemy troops, machine gun emplacements — less the three he had eliminated — and tank destroyers dug-in deeper in the woods. It was exactly the sort of information scouts were supposed to bring back. Robbins grinned as he listened to Biddle's matter-of-fact account of his extraordinary adventure, amused that all he now seemed to want was food — ideally, Robbins imagined, a wedge of Mom's chocolate cake and a bottle of milk. He told the scout the attack would resume in a few hours.

With daybreak approaching, Biddle sat against a tree overlooking the field. He used the knife strapped to his calf to open a can of C-rations. He could see two dead Germans from the downed plane lying in the field. The bodies had been stripped of their fur-lined, black-leather flight jackets, watches, rings, pistols — one had a *Luger*, the other a *Walther* P38 — and anything of souvenir value. It seemed that he had barely closed his eyes when Robbins called for B Company to saddle up.

"Biddle out front," he hollered. The scout's face showed that he thought his time in the woods merited a reprieve from walking point. Robbins smiled. "Biddle, you're so damn lucky we want you out there."

The renewed attacks by the 517th jumped off on schedule at 0815. An hour earlier, luck had literally come looking for Boyle when the commander of a tank destroyer sauntered across the bridge to see if he could be of help. Boyle assured him that he most definitely could, but first Boyle would go through the proper channels to get permission from the much-maligned colonel from the 84th, who readily agreed. Boyle's tactical plan was straight from a textbook: firing from across the river, the tank destroyer would throw a round into a house the instant before the paratroopers stormed it, shooting at anything that moved, while others behind the house stood ready to cut down any escaping enemy. As one house was secured they would move to the next one, and the next one — there were perhaps ten houses to clear — until the Germans were flushed from the village. There was still the matter of the Mk IV's lingering in the orchard at the bend in the road, but they also would be dealt with.

At 0900, Howze was surprised by the sudden appearance of Brigadier General Doyle Hickey, then jolted when Hickey announced the purpose of his visit: "By order of General Rose, I am in command here." For the first time in his military career, Howze had been relieved of his post. Hickey tried to soften the blow by adding the word "temporarily," though it's doubtful Howze heard it or was comforted if he did. The 52 year-old Arkansas-born Hickey was the commanding general of Combat Command A, and universally respected within the 3rd Armored Division. Rose had only recently gotten him back from another Army corps where CCA had helped to plug a hole in the vicinity of Eupen. Hickey had met Howze only a few times and had been favorably impressed. Now, as he was briefed on the situation, Hickey privately questioned why Rose had sent him on this mission. From what he was hearing, Howze was on top of the situation. After half an hour he got up to leave.

"I'm going down to the 83rd Reconnaissance area," he said, referring to Task Force Kane. "That looks like the hot spot."

A few minutes later Rose himself appeared, his manner brusque and peremptory. He began pelting Howze with questions. What was the status in Hotton? Were the woods clear? Had Hogan's supplies gotten through? Howze answered that he had not heard from Boyle or Fraser since they had resumed the attack, nor had he heard from Hogan. Rose told him to contact Hogan again.

"Vital that you notify us when supplies arrive," Howze radioed. "Trying to get air support for you."

As he paced the room, Rose informed his subordinate that the 290th Regiment of the 75th Infantry Division was en route to them, representing an infusion of another thousand men. Howze was unfamiliar with the outfit. Rose curtly explained that the 75th had only recently landed in Europe. He instructed Howze to notify Fickessen they were on the way.

"The 290th Infantry Regiment is relieving Hotton," he radioed. "No 3AD personnel will leave Hotton until ordered by commanding general."

At 1030, they heard planes overhead and rushed outside. Howze counted eight C-47 transport planes heading in a southeasterly direction, presumably hauling Hogan's supplies that Rose mistakenly believed had already been dropped. Just then they received word that Fraser's force was meeting little resistance, and that Boyle was making progress in Hotton.

In fact, Fraser had destroyed the two enemy tank destroyers that Biddle had spotted, and was on the cusp of clearing the woods between *Quatre Bras* and Hotton. Since resuming the attack two hours earlier, Biddle had killed another dozen Germans, most of them while firing his M-1 from the same position. Finally, at 1125, Rose and Howze got the news that Boyle and Fraser had made contact in Hotton. The two forces had joined up at the *Chapel des Anges* prayer hut just below the tree line at the edge of the village. Fraser later summarized the morning's action.

"Colonel Boyle attacked toward me and I attacked toward him. I knew he would be leading his forces and I would recognize him and not shoot him. I was the lead man of my forces and knew he would not shoot me. We cleaned up the Germans in the middle."

Nearby, scores of German dead had been left behind, many of them boys too young to shave, laid out in rows on the frost-covered ground. Paratroopers walked through their frozen ranks kicking the bodies to be sure they were dead. One was laying under a piece of tarp, his new boots exposed. Barney Hekkala lifted the tarp.

"He was a very live German with his weapon at his side," Hekkala recalled. "I was about to shoot him when a fellow trooper came up and said, 'Let me shoot him. I just took this pistol off a dead Kraut and I want to see how it works.' Well, the trooper couldn't figure out how the safety worked on the pistol, while the German was on his knees praying. About that time, another of our guys came running over. 'Don't shoot him! Headquarters wants some prisoners to interrogate.'" Said Hekkala, "Someone heard that German's prayers."

With the enemy purged from the village, Jack Warden's small force took up positions along the connector road. Two wiremen saw them and emerged from a home near the sawmill, unaware they had been presumed dead since the night of the 22nd. Bill Boyle set a roadblock above the prayer chapel where the road hooked toward Soy, then outposted his remaining men in the thick brush along the eastern shoulder of the road between there and *Quatre Bras*, where he set a second roadblock.

Directly across from this thin defensive line, barely visible through the trees, was the hill *La Roumière*. It was to this high ground that the enemy had retreated, and where Rose was convinced they were preparing to counterattack.

*   *   *

Rose and Howze were reviewing their troop list and available armor when Colonel Carl Duffner arrived in Soy. Duffner was the commanding officer of the 290th Regimental Combat Team, part of the 75th Infantry Division. He told them that he had two battalions of infantry heading their way. This substantial infusion of troops was what Rose had long been waiting for to relieve his men in Hotton. With the village now secured he focused on two intertwined objectives, namely, attacking the enemy and rescuing Sam Hogan's surrounded and fuel-starved force. Getting to Hogan or getting him out was all the more urgent since learning that the supply train of C-47s seen heading his way that morning had missed their drop despite a cloudless sky.

The 75th was a green unit, having debarked in Le Havre, France, less than two weeks earlier. Not only was it the newest American division to be committed to battle in Europe, it was also the youngest with an average troop age upon activation of just 21-years old, hence their nickname "the Diaper Division." Like everyone else, the men of the 290th were sleep-deprived and exhausted, especially the officers. Since crossing into a hostile and chaotic Belgium by train on December 20th, they had been packed into open trucks and moved in freezing rain from one nameless village to another, their orders constantly changing. In just the last twenty-four hours Duffner's 3rd Battalion had moved twice, each time laboriously digging in and setting defenses. Now they were assembled at a wooded crossroads north of Hotton. Although highly trained, not one of the 3,104 officers and enlisted men in the 290th had seen combat.

At 1225, Rose departed for his new CP near the village of Bomal – as always, perilously close to the action. A minute later, Howze took Duffner on a "reconnaissance" of the area to be turned over to the 290th. It wasn't a reconnaissance in the sense of gathering new information, but more of a courtesy tour to acquaint Duffner with who and what was where. It also allowed both officers to inspect the aftermath of four days of intense fighting. In the field below Soy they saw the tanks lost by Captain Mize and the crumpled Junker Ju 88 shot down the night before, its nose buried in the earth. From *Quatre Bras* they saw at least four enemy armored vehicles and clusters of German dead. Up ahead they passed two still smoldering Jagdpanser IV tank destroyers and saw Boyle's paratroopers spreading out along the road facing *La Roumière*. And in Hotton they saw a once bucolic village ravaged by war with homes reduced to rubble and charred vehicles seemingly everywhere. Howze did not cross the bridge to confer with Fickessen or pause to meet with Anderson. Instead, the two officers drove north on Barvaux Road toward Ny, and from there uphill to Soy. The trip took exactly an hour.

There was a stack of messages awaiting Howze when he returned to his desk. A third supply drop to Task Force Hogan was scheduled for 1345. Seven tank destroyers were en route to

Soy. Task Forces Kane and Orr to the northeast were taking heavy casualties. And Bill Boyle was on his way in with a dozen prisoners. He arrived there around 1400 hours. Howze congratulated him on a job well done, then directed him to a barn where he and his men could rest up. They would remain in Soy as his reserve, but for the moment he was through with them.

Boyle's rest was short-lived. At 1600 he was back in Howze's CP. Duffner was also there, along with 3rd Battalion's executive officer, Major Baskin, a lieutenant from one of the 290th's anti-tank platoons, and various unit commanders. Conspicuously absent was 3rd Battalion's commanding officer, Lt. Colonel Roland Gleszer, who had just arrived in Hotton and was apparently unaware of the meeting. Howze went straight to the point.

"Here's the proposition. The 290th is attached to me effective at once. We will push on to the high ground tonight."

The change in orders attaching the 290th to Howze's Combat Command Reserve, as opposed to relieving CCR in the Soy-Hotton sector, meant that Howze – on Rose's short leash – would command the operation.

For the next half hour he laid out the plan of attack. Duffner's 2nd Battalion would assemble near Wy, just through the woods from Melines, and attack up the wooded north slope of *La Roumière*. Two rifle companies of 3rd Battalion – K and L – would assemble in Ny and attack up the front or western slope of the hill, with I Company in reserve in Hotton. The line of departure for the attack by K and L Companies would be the ridgeline on Soy Road defended by Boyle's paratroopers. Time of attack was 1800, less than two hours away.

Colonel Duffner was nearly dumbstruck by what he heard. He had seen the aftermath of the fighting before the 290th arrived, and suggested that it was reckless to throw green troops against a battle-hardened enemy, especially at night. Moreover, his troops had hardly slept in three days; their ammunition trucks had not yet arrived; the radios were set to different frequencies; and his officers would have little if any opportunity to reconnoiter the area before dark.

"This is the most hurry-up job yet," Howze conceded. "But it must be done . . . . No sense to try to change any more radios now. Let's get going."

Major Baskin also voiced concern, noting that 3rd Battalion's commanding officer, Roland Gleszer, as well as the company commanders and platoon leaders, still needed to be briefed; K and L Companies had to get from their present position at the road junction to the new assembly point in Ny; and once there they would need to make preparations for battle. It couldn't be done by 1800 hours.

Howze knew the officers' concerns were legitimate, but he also knew that Rose would be breathing down his neck until the attack began. He ordered them to get it done as quickly as possible. Colonel Boyle, who had said nothing during the briefing, volunteered to take Baskin on a reconnaissance of the area while there was still light.

No sooner had the meeting finished when the Commanding General of the 75th Infantry Division, Fay Prickett, entered the room, requiring Howze to run through the briefing again. Under more convivial circumstances the two men might have discovered they had much in common: both came from distinguished lines of West Pointers – Prickett was fourth generation – and each was father to a tribe of girls. This wasn't the occasion. Prickett was similarly alarmed by what was being asked of the 290th.

"This is a pretty hard mission," he said. "This is the first time they have been committed."

"I know it, sir," said Howze. "But I'm not giving the order."

When this meeting broke up, Howze sent his liaison officer to Hotton with an overlay map of the operation to give to Lt. McDonald, who was to deliver it to General Bolling in Marche. Bolling had his hands full. His 84th had engaged the 116th Panzer Division in the corridor between Hotton and Marche, and he had just learned the 84th would provide artillery support for the attack on *La Roumière*.

At 1955, Howze reported to Rose that preparations for the attack were proceeding slowly. Still feeling the sting from having been "temporarily" relieved of his command that morning, he proffered an excuse for the delay. "This is their first night attack and they didn't arrive until dark. Everything quiet here." At 2117, he reported that preparations were still dragging due to the radio problems Duffner had foreseen. "Because they had no communication, one battalion has not arrived – they were lost. Communication is not straightened out yet."

In fact, K and L Companies were lost due to a chain of miscommunications and mishaps. When Baskin did not find L Company's commanding officer, Captain Dave Clagett, at the battalion assembly point, he radioed the 290th's personnel officer in Hotton to find him and have him report to Soy. The S-1 was able reach Clagett by radio but mistakenly told him to meet Baskin in Hotton, while neglecting to tell him that K and L Companies were moving to Ny. Clagett went to Hotton as instructed, and not finding Baskin returned to the now deserted road junction. Meanwhile, Baskin went to Ny assuming everyone was there, and when they weren't began driving around looking for them. He finally found the two companies two miles away heading in the wrong direction. He led them to Ny, where they arrived at 2200 after marching five hours with full packs.

Around 2245, 3rd Battalion's mess trucks pulled into Ny. The men were glad to see them as they had missed breakfast that morning. They were queuing at the mess trucks when Brigadier General Gerald Mickle drove up. The Assistant Division Commander of the 75th had just met with Howze, who almost certainly shared his frustration with 3rd Battalion's snail's pace progress. Mickle assured him that he would get the show going. Lt. Colonel Gleszer was standing near one of the kitchen trucks when Mickle pulled up. Mickle told him to close the chow line and prepare his companies to attack immediately.

"General, these men haven't had anything but K-rations all day," said Gleszer.

"Colonel, you're a West Pointer," Mickle snapped. "Can't you obey an order?"

Baskin, Clagett and Andy Robble, the commanding officer of K Company, overheard the exchange. Gleszer waved them over. Baskin informed the general that their ammunition trucks had not yet arrived, suggesting there was still time for the men to eat. Mickle told them to distribute whatever ammo they had and move out.

K and L Companies left Ny around 2300, Robble and Clagett giving the attack orders to their platoon leaders while marching. Above Ny the road curved and leveled off, leading the hungry troops past the twisted forms of German dead and burning vehicles.

At *Quatre Bras* they spread out along Soy Road, their line of departure. Boyle's paratroopers were struck that the fresh-faced soldiers still had rifles slung and what appeared to be very little ammunition. The standard combat load was one bandolier containing twelve eight-round clips, yet these men had half that or less. By comparison, the paratroopers each carried at least two more bandoliers as well as extra grenades. Here and there they offered the men of the 290th some of theirs, which strangely was declined. Nineteen year-old Gil Nelson of L Company recalled that Colonel Duffner addressed his troops from atop a half-track prior to jump off. "Tonight your stomachs may be empty but tomorrow, the birthday of our Lord, your hearts will be flush with victory."

At 2315, Howze reported to Rose that the attack had started. Now into his third pack of cigarettes for the day, Howze's thoughts returned to Task Force Hogan in Marcouray. In his latest messages, Hogan reported that they had repelled an enemy patrol, capturing two, and that a lone German soldier had come forward to surrender, telling his captors that he was "tired of war." At one minute past midnight, Christmas Day, Howze radioed back.

"Two attempts at resupplying you will be made tomorrow. Fighters will accompany transports so that you can talk them over the town. Have large circle of panels displayed. Also have arty prepared to mark with violet or green smoke. Which do you have the most of?"

La Roumière as seen from Soy.

View from the treeline on *La Roumière*, looking toward *Quatre Bras*.

The crest of *La Roumière*.

The barn in Soy where Boyle's paratroopers rested after clearing Hotton.

08.

IT IS EASY TO BECOME DISORIENTED IN THE ARDENNES. The vast stretches of forest and undulating hills, the outcroppings of rock, rivers and streams, the tucked away valleys – all can seem indistinguishable to those unfamiliar with the engulfing landscape. Night compounds the phenomenon.

When they crossed their line of departure on Soy Road, the two companies of 3rd Battalion could have descended straight downhill through the woods then uphill to *La Roumière*. To save time, Clagett and Robble marched their men down the road to Melines about a quarter-mile where it curved sharply, entering the woods there. From here the terrain sloped steeply about 150 feet to a narrow valley traversed by a meandering stream, on the far side of which the woods rose again to a road connecting the villages of Melines and Werpin along the base of the hill. Across the road a wide meadow crept upwards about 450 yards to the densely wooded crest. It was here that the Germans had dug-in, their positions well camouflaged with excellent fields of grazing fire over the meadow below.

Dave Clagett reached the jump off point below the Melines-Werpin road shortly after midnight. Nearly pitch dark despite a rising moon, the temperature was in the low twenties and falling. He had lost contact with two of his three platoons, as well as with Andy Robble's entire K Company. Unable to raise them by radio, he dispatched runners to find them. When they didn't return, he started up the slope with the one platoon he had, hoping to join up with the others on the hill.

Newly designated scout Gil Nelson was out front. He was surprisingly calm, his confidence bolstered by the honor of being tapped for the job and because his squad sergeant had told him the assault would be just like the training exercises they had practiced in Wales. There was no sign of the enemy as they started out, the only sound that of their crunching footsteps announcing their advance up the frost-covered meadow. Nelson was nearing the tree line when he heard a single shot and felt a bullet zip past his ear. Like everyone else, he had seen the German dead along the road to *Quatre Bras* and the burning armored vehicles and had been moved by Duffner's florid talk of victory. Yet now his mind duped him into believing that all of this was another training problem.

"Sarge, that was a live one!" he whispered back. "Shouldn't we do this right?" By this he meant that the platoon should stay back until he had scouted the woods.

"Damn it, just go, Oz!" said the sergeant.

The tree line above them came alive with small arms fire. No one in Nelson's squad fired back, at least initially and then half-heartedly. He dropped to the ground and tried to bury himself in the earth. His sergeant cried out, "I've been hit!"

Trembling with fear, Nelson belly-crawled to the wounded sergeant and dragged him to an outcrop of rock. German mortar began falling in the meadow, scattering the men, some of them running into the enemy-held woods seeking cover. Deciding their position was untenable, Clagett ordered the platoon to withdraw. After a while the firing ebbed. Shifting clouds periodically eclipsed the moon. Nelson waited for such an interlude, then hoisted the sergeant onto his shoulders and carried him to safety.

* * *

NOBODY IN SOY KNEW WHAT WAS HAPPENING – NOT GLESZer, not Duffner, and certainly not Howze. This was because none of the K and L Company radios were operational, and none of the runners dispatched by Clagett and Robble to find the other had made contact. The first news Howze received, at 0500, was that the leading elements of both forces – 2nd Battalion attacking from Wy and 3rd Battalion attacking from the Melines-Werpin road – were "on the objective." Howze forwarded the news to Rose. Half an hour later he had to correct his report after learning that 2nd Battalion was just getting to Wy, and 3rd Battalion was only now organizing at the base of the hill, which K Company and the missing platoons from L Company had finally found.

They jumped off at first light, L Company to the left and abreast of K Company. The attack was not preceded by artillery or mortar fire on the hill out of concern that the men who had unwittingly run into the enemy-held woods during the first assault would become casualties of friendly fire. The fog had lifted and the sky was clearing.

"Do you know how much cover we had?" Robble wrote later. "Absolutely none! This attack was to be made uphill in an open field, a cow pasture with hardly a bush, let alone any trees or other cover. This was a suicide mission."

Another soldier likened the front slope to the belly of a

huge whale. The enemy was silent. Dave Clagget went up the far left side of the hill with his radioman, ahead of the others, and entered the tree line at the top.

"As we crossed it we came under machine gun fire. We both hit the ground and commenced firing at what we thought was the source. A machine gun firing from our flank sent a burst across Bishop's chest, killing him, and hit me in the left hip and thigh." Clagett crawled to a slight depression that he hoped would give him some defilade from the machine gun that had cut him down.

Lieutenant Dutch Meier was approaching the tree line in the middle of the field when a German shouted in perfect English, "Hey you, down there!" Meier answered, "Hey yourself, you sonuvabitch!" Turning, he saw that his platoon had stopped advancing. He stood up, waving them forward. "Get the hell up here with the rest of us!" Just then he realized he had been shot. "Ah, shit! Get a medic! I'm bleeding to death!"

Andy Robble was near the top of the meadow when he passed Lieutenant John Peirson of L Company. Everybody in 3rd Battalion knew Peirson for the simple reason that, at thirty-two, he was considered ancient by Diaper Division metrics. There was also a certain patrician air about him, nothing snooty, but reflective of his prominent banking-family background, a Yale education and a resumé that included a stint at *Fortune* magazine. In the two years since enlisting, Peirson had exchanged 432 love letters and telegrams with his wife, and had recently become a father. Robble heard the siren scream of an incoming shell and dove for a tree. When he looked up there was a crater where he had seen Peirson an instant before. The shell burst, a direct hit, had so disarticulated his fellow officer that his left forearm would be the only intact bone later recovered; even his dog tags were gone. Robble had no time to contemplate what had just happened.

"We really didn't have a fighting chance," he recalled. "The enemy opened up with rifle and machine gun fire . . . . As I hit the dirt I got hit across both shoulders, shearing off part of my left shoulder blade. The bullet also hit part of my vertebrae and practically paralyzed me. I couldn't move. The only thing I could do was to send my runner to get Lieutenant Ellis on my right flank and tell him to move on up through the wooded area."

As he lay there bleeding, Robble heard a chorus of cries all around him. "Medic! Medic!" He heard German voices sing out "Doctor, eh!" followed by bursts from an *MP40* – popularly known as a "burp gun" – as the wounded were executed.

Lieutenant Paul Ellis was leading his platoon uphill through the trees along the right boundary of the pasture. The incoming fire was high, showering him with wood splinters and pine needles. He and two others made it to the top, where, twenty yards to their left, they saw four Germans firing down the hill. They lobbed grenades at the machine gun nest, killing all four. One of his men asked Ellis if he should bayonet them to make sure they were dead. The Germans had suffered massive head wounds. Ellis told him it was unnecessary. The other soldier turned to him.

"Lieutenant, you see the boots on those sons-of-bitches?" he said, admiring their new leather boots.

For a moment, the 22 year-old Clemson graduate thought

the soldier would plop down and swap his own four-buckle rubber boots, which were waterproof but heavy, for a pair off one of the dead. By now the Americans were out or nearly out of ammunition. Sensing their fire had dwindled, Germans entrenched deeper in the woods rushed forward with guns blazing. Ellis decided their best exit was straight down the front slope of the hill. They almost made it to the Melines-Werpin road.

"Gerwitz running beside me was hit twice in the back, killing him instantly," Ellis remembered. "I turned to check on him and saw there was nothing I could do. As I started toward the ditch again I was hit in the right leg. I managed to crawl the remaining distance to the barbed wire fence and into the ditch."

He was luckier than most. Sergeant Joe Harlukowicz was hit twice.

"We started up the hill when I got one helluva wallop in the upper right arm. It probably caused me to stumble because I found myself face down. In no time at all a medic was alongside me . . . . Just then a bullet tore through my left forearm and upper left chest. With some fervor I said 'Son of a bitch! You better get the hell out of here. They're trying to pick you off.' He had lost his helmet and asked for mine . . . I heard a bullet go 'pfft' overhead. Another 'pfft.' And a third. Again 'pfft.' Someone had me in his sights."

By 1000 hours the second assault on *La Roumière* was over. Everyone who could get off the hill had, leaving scores of wounded to freeze in the open pasture because they could not be reached due to sniper fire. Others had fallen in the thick brush on the edges of the pasture and could not be seen. Jake Weisinger was among the last to be hit. The 20 year-old second lieutenant was at the base of the hill when a sniper round clipped his spine and traveled down his leg, the seventh officer – out of eleven on the field – to go down. Dave Clagett, already shot five times and drifting between unconsciousness and sleep, felt the draft from a passing bullet. A moment later a second bullet tore through the calf of his right leg. He turned his head in the direction of the fire and saw a German gun crew motioning to him to surrender. His legs useless, he crawled fifty feet to their position. One of the soldiers who had shot him inspected his wounds, then tied off his left leg with a tourniquet. It would save Clagett's life.

* * *

HOWZE HAD THE UNENVIABLE DUTY OF TELLING GENERAL Rose that the situation was "not good." He wasn't referring to the casualty count, of which he knew nothing, but simply that the enemy still held the hill. 3rd Battalion had been all but slaughtered in their attempt to seize the objective from the front, while 2nd Battalion, which was supposed to have attacked up the left slope ten hours earlier, was bogged down in Wy against enemy tanks and infantry. The dismal result reinforced Howze's belief that the enemy was present in large numbers and was preparing to strike soon. Rose answered that he wanted "maximum effort as soon as possible." To Howze this meant committing more men to the fight. He considered turning again to Boyle's 517th, beat up as they were, but looked instead to I Company in Hotton, where things were relatively quiet. Over the next two hours a new plan was formed to hit the enemy from three sides: what was left of K and L Companies would resume the attack from the front; 2nd Battalion would attack from the left; and I Company, supported by a platoon of tank destroyers, would attack the hill from the right. To get to their jump off position, I Company would march to Hampteau, cross the Ourthe and proceed through Werpin to the right slope of the hill. Jack Fickessen saw them pulling out and radioed Howze.

"Company from the 75th here with us is leaving. When do we get out of the electric chair?"

"Will move your headquarters here sometime today," Howze announced.

Around noon Duffner reported that 2nd Battalion was still tied up in Wy. Howze summoned Bill Boyle.

"The picture's bad," said Howze. "We must take these objectives. Start moving now and get this battalion up there. We are faced with a major German counterattack and if we don't get this high ground the war will last a long time. Can I aid this attack with tanks?"

"We have tanks in there," said Boyle.

"Jump off at 1430. It is now 1303. At 1440, hit them the damnedest lick they ever had."

To get to their line of attack, Boyle's men marched north on Soy Road a short distance, then proceeded southeast and downhill on a narrow logging path through a section of woods known as *La Foret Melines*. At the bottom they came to a spongy half-frozen bog called *Nébovâ*, a French-Walloon name meaning "valley of no good." Across from Nébovâ the wooded left slope climbed 300 yards at a 34-degree angle to the crest of the hill. It was a daunting climb for even the fittest hikers, but especially so for men weighted down with weapons and ammunition while being shot at.

The time of the attack was pushed back slightly when I Company encountered small arms fire in Werpin, the shots coming from behind a towering statue of the Virgin Mary. The troops scattered and then did what they had been trained to do, moving house-to-house in search of the enemy, capturing five Germans. By 1500 hours, everybody was in position, radios working, when the hilltop exploded in an intense artillery bombardment. Gil Nelson witnessed red and green smoke marking the target area. The artillery preparation lasted five minutes, an eternity for the Germans on top of the hill. Hours earlier, a semi-conscious Dave Clagett had been carried by stretcher to the German command post set deep in the woods. Now, under the horrific bombardment, his life was saved a second time when a grenadier dragged him to an empty slit trench to protect him from tree bursts. Across from him in a nearby foxhole a German officer was staring at him intently. This went on long enough for Clagett to worry that the officer had decided to either interrogate him or kill him. The officer abruptly scrambled over to Clagett's trench, pointing at the American's rank insignia.

"Are you a captain?" said the German.

Clagett nodded. "Yes, I am a captain."

"Me too!" said the German, his eyes wild. "For six years I have been a captain!" With that he crab-crawled back to his own foxhole, leaving Clagett to foggily conclude that promotions were hard to come by in both of their armies.

At 1513, Boyle radioed Howze that they were receiving

heavy machine gun and mortar fire. 2nd Battalion's F Company, standing by in reserve in Soy, was now committed to also attack up the left side of the hill. Boyle, meanwhile, had brought his own artillery forward observer, who directed the fire to land "right smack in front of us." The artillery called in by the 290th was less precise, some of shells landing among the wounded on the front slope. K Company's Andy Robble, bleeding into the earth since dawn, caught shrapnel in his left leg. Joe Harlukowicz was spread-eagled when a marble-sized ball opened his boot, his third wound of the day. The misfires had a paralyzing effect on the men watching from the Melines-Werpin road. When the shelling stopped they were commanded to move out; no one did. Again the command and again no one budged. A young private stood up. "What the hell are we waiting for, Christmas?" He moved out and the rest followed.

At 1620, Howze radioed to both Boyle and Fraser pleading for aggression. "Drive on to objective. It is desperate," he told Boyle. "Push on, it is desperate," he echoed to Fraser. The impetus for these distress calls was Sam Hogan.

* * *

CHRISTMAS MORNING IN MARCOURAY WAS QUIET AND COLD, the temperature in the high teens and the sky clear. The frost covered hills to the north and east appeared snowy. At 0735, Sam Hogan radioed that he had eight rounds of green smoke to mark his position for the promised supply drop. Howze replied that he should use yellow smoke grenades unless he could place the green in or close to the village. Hogan answered that he would mark with green. At 0925, he was instructed to stand by on a different radio frequency so that he could talk directly with the pilots, who would tell him when to "smoke the target." Half an hour later, without explanation, Hogan recommended that the supply mission be aborted. Howze forwarded the message to Rose, who wanted verification that it had been sent by Hogan. At 1125, the mission was cancelled. Three minutes later, Hogan requested "any information you can on enemy and friendly troops from Hotton up river on both sides." The message meant one thing: Hogan wanted to break out on foot.

The decision, however, wasn't his to make; it was General Rose's. Rose wasn't keen on leaving behind weapons and equipment that might later be used against him, but he recognized that he wasn't standing in Hogan's boots either. He considered the situation. Three attempts to resupply had failed. Even if they could supply Hogan soon, they couldn't drop enough fuel to last him more than a day. It now appeared that it would take at least that long to clear *La Roumière*, which would drive yet more Germans toward Marcouray. He authorized the Texan to do what he had to do to save his men.

Howze and Hogan exchanged messages all afternoon.

"One dead, fourteen wounded, three missing," Hogan reported. "Effective strength 467."

"Regiments of 116th Panzer Division on main and small roads and in towns on both sides of the river," said Howze. "Ninth Panzer Division in area of March. Successful escapes to west then north have been made off roads."

"Do we hold Soy?"

"We do hold Soy."

"Heading toward Soy without helmets, faces blacked. Officer strength 26."

Around 1700 hours, a squad of elite Pathfinders from the 509th wandered into Howze's CP. Rested after fighting alongside Don Fraser's men at *Quatre Bras*, they were looking for something to do. Young, fit, and seasoned combat veterans, they exuded a relaxed confidence that allowed them to approach those of higher rank on an equal level and get away with it. Overhearing the discussion about Hogan's breakout, they volunteered to help: "Hey, Colonel, we'll fetch those fellas for ya." Howze couldn't help but smile. He radioed Hogan.

"Six commandos en route along high ground and woods east of river to assist. Do not wait for them. Destroy equipment. Password is hornet-stings."

Hogan had already put his men to work destroying anything that could be of use to the enemy. They could have burned everything, but the smoke would have given away both their position and their intention, setting them up as targets for the German artillery and an attack. Instead, Hogan ordered his men to drain the oil from all vehicles, pour sugar in the gas tanks, and then run the motors until they locked up. Weapons were field-stripped and the parts dropped into water wells, along with all remaining ammunition and grenades. Radios were pulverized and vacuum tubes smashed. The German prisoner shot in the back of the head three days earlier was buried under some shrubs lest he be discovered before they could escape. Hogan's dead tanker was buried in an isolated and readily identifiable spot so that the body could be retrieved. The matter of Hogan's 14 wounded was resolved when one of his officers volunteered to stay behind, taking a chance the Germans would treat them humanely. Finally, the men were ordered to blacken their faces and hands — chimney soot or axel grease worked equally well — and to remove their helmets and anything else that might make noise as they made their way out. Under no circumstances, Hogan told them, were they to bring rifles or pistols since one nervously fired shot could spell doom for everyone. They would move out in a single column in groups of twelve as soon as it was dark.

At 1800, Howze radioed Hogan for the last time: "Good luck, God bless you." He then notified all unit commanders to be on the lookout. "Hogan will head for Soy tonight dismounted. Route along river east side through woods to point 404867 to Soy. No helmets and faces black. They know the password."

Jack Fickessen, meanwhile, had arrived in Soy with his 23rd Engineers, grateful to be out of the electric chair. Bill Rodman had moved his men to Barvaux. This left John Anderson the senior-ranking officer in Hotton. The village was still being shelled from across the river by Johannes Bayer's guns, harassing fire intended, ironically enough, to impede reinforcements to Bolling's 84th. Rose told Howze to make sure that all remaining troops in Hotton understood that only he (Rose) or Anderson was authorized to blow the bridge. On the other hand, if General Bolling wanted to blow it, that was fine, too.

"Captain Anderson is in command. See that all platoon leaders understand that he is the boss. See that he has everything on the right side of the bridge. The 84th can blow it if they want to."

* * *

By dusk, all elements of the 290th were on the top of the hill, albeit disorganized and jumpy. Gil Nelson saw only dead Germans, thought the battle was over and took a swig of cognac from a canteen. The 517th was on the left side of the hill when they began taking fire from three sides. Bill Boyle realized it was coming from the 290th. He marched into the open waving his arms. "Cease fire! Cease fire! I'm Colonel Boyle! Cease fire!" McConley Bird of F Company recalled the scene.

"It was getting dark and we thought we were getting a counterattack by the Germans. But it was the Colonel and 517th troops and Company F firing at each other. The Colonel took charge and told all the men to close in around a big tree. I don't remember the number, maybe 50 or 75. He had the artillery forward observer calling artillery fire within 50 to 100 yards on all four sides. Some of the shells fell pretty close to us around the tree. Then the Colonel said line up in single file and hold on to the cartridge belt of the man in front of you. He then called the BAR [Browning automatic rifle] man out front with him and ordered all of us to be quiet and led us over the top of the hill to the edge of a cleared field . . . . There was a squad of Germans. The Colonel challenged them in German and they didn't respond. He had the BAR man open fire on them and they ran off the hill like horse drawn artillery was behind them."

Boyle radioed Howze.

"Situation: we have one-third of it, but don't have the forward slope of the hill. I ran into Company I and Company F. I got a platoon up there. The commanding officer doesn't know anything about the rest of them . . . . He has about 30-40 men. I got a bit of fire before this creek. All we met then was a few snipers. Company I is now with me. I have also 15 men from Company L."

"Can you get down there and get this forward slope organized?" said Howze.

"Plenty rugged tonight. Those kids are all scared stiff. Right at the moment they're pretty unsettled. I don't think it's Jerry firing."

"My orders are to push on the forward slope. Get ahold of those two commanders and tell them to get their men and push off. They're the commanders down there."

"I'll get them out there if I place every man by myself."

In fact, Boyle had seen only the one officer from the 290th, and he had vanished. He sent Fraser to personally report this to Howze.

"Colonel, there are no officers up there," said Fraser. "No one's commanding these kids and I don't know how to contact their CO."

"I sure as hell can get him," said Howze, walking over to his newly installed switchboard. "Get me Colonel Gleszer," he said to his message clerk. A moment later the clerk looked up. "They say he's asleep, Colonel."

"You tell them to wake him up and that he is to report here immediately!"

Don Fraser was still there when Gleszer entered Howze's CP.

"I thought for sure Colonel Howze was gonna have a stroke on the spot. I've rarely seen a man that mad. 'Goddammit, what are you doing sleeping?' he said to Gleszer. 'Your men are up there on that hill with no one telling them what to do! Colonel, you are relieved as of now and you are never to set foot in this CP again! Now leave!'"

"I was so embarrassed for the guy I wanted to melt through the floor," said Fraser. "Howze was completely justified in doing what he did, but it was an awful thing to watch. Gleszer just kinda stood there. He was stunned. 'You're dismissed, Colonel!' Howze told him. Then he told me to go back and tell Colonel Boyle he was in command of all the forces on that hill. I was glad to get outta there."

Meanwhile, deep in the woods atop *La Roumière*, Dave Clagett opened his eyes to see an American soldier standing over him, his rifle pointed at Clagett's chest. He was still lying in the slit trench where his captors had dragged him during the artillery bombardment a few hours earlier. The Germans had fled the hill without bothering to kill him.

"Come out of there, Jerry," said the soldier, assuming the wounded Clagett was a German wearing GI fatigues who had been left for dead. The nearly bloodless Clagett spoke in a barely audible whisper.

"You can't shoot me," he said. "I am the Ambassador from Tasmania." The soldier didn't know Tasmania from Toledo but decided the voice was distinctly American. He had Clagett put on a stretcher and loaded onto the back of a tank, which ferried him off the hill to the nearest aid-station. The next morning he was taken to a hospital in Liège, then moved to a hospital in Paris, and from there to a hospital in England. His war was over.

148

Captain Dave Clagett
recuperating in
England, 1945.

Lt. John Peirson,
killed on *La Roumière*
Christmas Day, 1944.

Troops of Task Force Hogan in Soy following their escape.

09.

AT 0120 ON DECEMBER 26TH, BOYLE REPORTED PROGRESS ON the hill.

150

"Left units practically in now . . . next unit to right will be in in about half hour. The right unit will take more time – will be in in three hours. Have not met any enemy opposition."

Boyle may not have met any enemy tanks or infantry, but the rear crest of the hill was taking artillery fire from German guns positioned to the east between the villages of Trinal and Beffe. Sergeant Charles Critchlow of the 517th, Mel Biddle's best friend since childhood, was killed around this time. So was 22 year-old Lieutenant Ken Jones, the only officer in the 290th to have survived three assaults up the hill's deadly front slope. The Kentucky native was the eighth officer from 3rd Battalion to fall, representing a casualty rate of 73 percent in a single day.

At 0445, the 290th reported that all troops were in position and were putting out mines and trip wire across all avenues of approach. Half an hour later eighteen men from Sam Hogan's task force emerged from the woods east of Werpin. Hogan's men dribbled in all morning, cold and tired and beaming with joy to have made it out. One man was accidentally shot in the leg by a soldier from the 290th. But Hogan was nowhere to be found. At 1420, he finally limped into Howze's CP assisted by his orderly and driver. Howze told Rose that he was there and okay. Rose ordered that he report to him immediately.

"Colonel, what kept you?"

Hogan considered responding with some heroic answer but decided to stick with the facts.

"My feet hurt, General."

* * *

GENERAL MATT RIDGWAY, STILL SHIFTING TROOPS LIKE chess pieces, decided he could use Boyle's men elsewhere now that the 290th held *La Roumière*. He pressed Rose to relieve them, Rose pressed Howze. At 0810, Howze radioed Boyle that his relief was on the way. Five hours later, a sleep-deprived and irritable Boyle was still on the hill. "The relief is not coming on worth a damn," he radioed, adding the magic words that he couldn't find the 290th colonel in charge. Howze told him to bring his paratroopers in.

When the 517th left Soy that afternoon, it marked the end of the battle for Hotton. In the four days since they had arrived, 11 paratroopers had been killed and 132 wounded, representing a casualty rate of approximately 28 percent. On the other side of the ledger, the 517th would be credited with 210 enemy killed, an unknown number wounded and 18 captured. Before leaving Soy, Boyle and Fraser dashed off a note to Howze, which they delivered to his CP.

FROM: Col. Boyle and Officers and Men
        of 1st Bn. 517th Prcht. C.T.

TO: Col. Howze and Officers and Men of
        His Command

Just a short informal note of Thanks and deep appreciation for the way you have taken care of us while in your Command.

These few days have been some of the hottest and most interesting fighting we have ever experienced.

This short workout has given us a new picture of the type of duties you perform and believe us when we say you have our sincere Admiration and Praise.

To have served with you all has been an Honor and a Pleasure and we hope to soldier again with you someday.

W. J. Boyle	Donald W. Fraser
Lt. Col., Inf.	Maj. 517 Prcht. Combat Team
Commanding	1st Bn. Exec.

The high cost of the battle had been shared. That morning only 53 men from Andy Robble's K Company answered roll call, having started out with approximately 170. Dave Clagett later estimated 3rd Battalion's losses at more than 250, including 81 dead, many of whom had frozen to death in the extreme cold with wounds that ordinarily would not have been fatal. The "very light" casualties reportedly suffered by the 3rd Armored troops actually totaled at least 87 killed, wounded and captured, plus an estimated 30 or more casualties among Captain Mize's tankers in the field below Soy. Losses suffered by the 509th Parachute Infantry Regiment are not known. Meanwhile, the fighting had shifted to the far side of the Ourthe River, where General Bolling's 84th Infantry Division was in the fight of its life against two Panzer divisions, including Johannes Bayer's forces that had slipped away from Hotton.

* * *

JACK WARDEN'S PLATOON WAS RELIEVED ON THE MORNING of December 27th, and a guide was sent to Hotton to lead John Anderson's headquarters company to a new assembly area in the village of Weris. In Soy, Howze was clearing out his command post when two men from McDonald's I & R platoon requested permission to speak with him. He looked up from his desk. They were there to nominate Chaplain Kraka for a Silver Star for his actions on the night of the 22nd when he armed himself with a Thompson sub-machine gun and fought as an infantryman. The two soldiers had personally witnessed the priest's actions. Howze blew a gasket.

"Are you nuts?" he bellowed. "Do you realize he could be court-martialed for this? Priests are non-combatants under the Geneva Convention! He could go to the brig, not to mention lose his collar!" Howze glanced at his line officer standing nearby, eyes wide. "Now listen up, everyone. We're all going to forget this conversation. It is not to leave this room. Is that understood?"

"Yes, sir," said the enlisted men.

Howze stood up from his desk after they had left, shaking his head. "Captain," he said, "I thought I'd heard it all."

He arrived in Weris around noon, where he devoted the balance of the day to paperwork. Much as he disliked it, it was a welcome respite from the crushing strain he had been under. That night, he slept outside his boots for the first time in a week.

He awoke the following morning a new man, and while still early took time to write his wife, enclosing the note of appreciation from Boyle and Fraser.

Dec 28
Belgium

Peggy Darling –

Wrote you a v-mail yesterday. It was all I had to write on.

Please put the enclosed note away for me. It came from the finest bunch of fighting men I've ever seen, and I want to keep it always. They practically saved my neck a few days ago.

Right this minute I'm in a nice warm Belgian house, have had a bath and a good night's sleep. I could use about six more of the sleep, but I'm feeling fine. I sure was tired last night.

It has become bitter cold. The ground is frozen solid. It's hell on front line troops.

I love you and love you and love you with all my heart and soul. I can't tell you how terribly I long for you and the monks.

Devotedly
Bobby

* * *

Although it would take another month to drive the German armies from Belgium, Hitler's ambition to seize Antwerp had been reduced to a pipe dream. In the first days of the offensive, 60,000 GIs had poured into the Ardennes to arrest the attack; by the end of the first week, 250,000 Americans had rolled in, about equal to the German forces arrayed against them; and before it was over, more than 600,000 GIs and airmen were involved in the fight. The six-week battle would cost America approximately 76,000 casualties, including more than 20,000 dead. German losses were conservatively estimated at 100,000 killed, wounded and captured.

When Johannes Bayer looked down on the village of Hotton from the *Sur les Hys* woods on the early morning of December 21st, his *Kampfgruppe* represented the deepest penetration by German forces into Belgium. Had he been able to capture the bridge intact, two things would have happened: first, he soon would have confronted Alexander Bolling's 84th Infantry Division, further stalling his advance to the Meuse River; and second, some portion of the German forces stacked up in the Ardennes looking for an opening to the west would have turned toward Hotton. The latter would not have been accomplished easily, if at all, since the fuel-starved Germans still had to defeat pockets of determined Americans in a dozen bridge villages and road centers such as Trois Ponts and Chevron, Grandmenil and Freineux, and of course Bastogne. All the while, the concentration of American troops aligned against them continued to mount.

Hotton was saved thanks in part to a large dose of luck. Bayer's hesitancy to commit more tanks and infantry to the first attack continues to puzzle given his initial assessment that the village was lightly defended. Luck visited again when Bayer waited nearly a day to renew the attack despite the directive that speed of movement was central to Hitler's plan. When he did attack in force the Americans were organized and stronger due to the infusion of Warden's small task force, the second 81-mm mortar crew and Charlie Bryson's tank destroyers. By this time the 517th was en route to Soy and soon to be joined by the 290th. The bloodiest fighting was still to come but an important gateway to the west had been closed.

In his later account of the ambush in Melines on the morning of December 21st, Edmund Socha wrote that Bayer remarked, "Ve vill be in Paris in vun veek." Notwithstanding that the German plan did not include a side trip to the City of Light, it is difficult to read Bayer's words as anything more than an attempt to bolster the confidence of his men. Certainly by the night of the 22nd when his battered force pulled back to LaRoche, losing yet more time, Bayer was recalculating the probability of reaching the Meuse. He never would get there, nor would any other German soldier until long after the war in Europe had been decided.

The Hotton action was a microcosm of the fierce combat across the Ardennes in those desperate first days, a universe in miniature of brave soldiers stubbornly engaged in what Winston Churchill famously called "the greatest battle in World War II."

Lt. Jack Warden *(kneeling, left)* with members of his taskforce.

Members of McDonald's I&R platoon after the battle,
joined by Sgt. Paul Copeland *(upper left)*.

Captain John Kraka

The Christmas card designed by Captain Phil Zulli and distributed to the troops of the 36th Armored Infantry Regiment before leaving Stolberg.

EPILOGUE

MIKE McDONALD would see another 121 days of combat in a blur of villages and cities. On February 4, 1945, he was back in Stolberg – where he had started out 47 days earlier – before pushing into the German heartland. On February 26th, he crossed the Roer River, then the Erft Canal. On March 6th, he picked up more "scratches" in Cologne, which was captured after a protracted door-to-door battle. On April 12th, his I&R platoon drew fire on the outskirts of Nordhausen, where Howze's troops opened the gates of a Nazi concentration camp. The next day, 1,000 Allied prisoners, mostly British, were liberated at Gerbstedt. On April 25th, the city of Dessau was taken following four days of intense fighting. For the men of the 3rd Armored Division, it was their last engagement of the war.

It turned out my father was not the giant killer I had read about in those early news articles. He did not knock out six tanks, nor did he single-handedly save Hotton. But he had contributed to the battle's outcome through a combination of skill and courage that was far from unique among the troops who fought there. He never thought of himself as a hero, and indeed, would have squirmed under the weight of such a lofty word. It was enough that he had done his job and had somehow survived.

In September 1945, he returned to Long Beach, New York, exactly two years after he had shipped off to England. His mother soon began pestering him to visit the wife of a soldier from his old unit in the hope that he could provide information about her husband, who had been listed as missing in action. Eager to put the war behind him, he resisted for several weeks; then, working his regimental contacts and other channels, it was determined that the husband – a replacement – had been killed by machine gun fire in the vicinity of Mauschback, Germany. One year later, my father married the widow of his fellow soldier in St. Patrick's Cathedral. Father John Kraka officiated at the ceremony.

MAURICE ROSE was killed on March 30, 1945, near Paderborn, Germany, after his jeep was pinned against a tree by a German King Tiger tank. Shot 14 times by the tank's commander while trying to surrender, the Army immediately launched an investigation under the direction of future Watergate prosecutor Leon Jaworski to determine whether a war crime had been committed. Investigators took into account that the shooting occurred at night in the midst of a heated battle, and that the tank commander, in a highly agitated state and in poor light, may have interpreted Rose's movement in lowering his arms to surrender his pistol as an act of aggression. By report dated June 1945, Colonel Jaworski concluded that the shooting was the result of "a combination of unfortunate circumstances" and recommended no further action.

Maurice Rose is today considered among the greatest generals in the history of armored warfare. He is buried in the American Military Cemetery in Margratan, Holland.

ROBERT HOWZE retired from the Army in 1962 as Major General, and died in 1983 following a car accident in

Carmel, California. In his eulogy, General Hamilton H. Howze wrote of his older brother: "Bobby felt always that the crescendo of his life came in the Battle of the Bulge . . . in the vicinity of Soy and Hotton, Belgium . . . this was what he had worked up to, trained for and lived for; he recognized it as the supreme test and, of course, very possibly the culminating one." In 1994, the citizens of Belgium honored Howze with a commemorative plaque affixed to a red brick house in Soy that served as his command post half a century earlier. Howze is buried beside his wife, Peggy, in the Army Cemetery at the Presidio of San Francisco.

HARVEY FRASER went on to become Professor of Mechanics at West Point, and subsequently earned a doctorate in Theoretical and Applied Mechanics from the University of Illinois. In 1965, he left the Army as a Brigadier General to become Dean of Engineering at the South Dakota School of Mines and Technology. Fraser retired in 1984 and lives in Colorado. Now 95, he considers his role in the actions of the 51st Engineers at Hotton and Trois Ponts, Belgium, to be his "finest hour."

After the war, BILL RODMAN earned a degree in animal husbandry at Virginia Polytechnic Institute, then managed a 1,700-acre farm growing alfalfa, soybeans and barley. In 1950, he underwent spinal surgery to repair the damage incurred from his fall in the Hotton schoolhouse, later joining the Foreign Agricultural Service where he spent the next 30 years promoting American farm products worldwide. He died in Virginia in 2010.

JOHN ANDERSON went home to South Carolina where he founded a successful construction company, became active in community and church affairs, and sang in a barbershop chorus. For the rest of his life he kept the lighter inscribed by Phil Zulli in a glass bookcase next to his desk, and remained in close touch with a cadre of officers from his old regiment. He died in 2002.

JACK FICKESSEN stayed in the Army and served with distinction during the Korean conflict. In 1968, he retired as Colonel and returned to his native Texas where he worked as civil engineer while cultivating a passion for photography. He died in 1992 and is buried at Fort Sam Houston Cemetery.

In June 1945, JOHN KRAKA received his last Efficiency Report from Colonel Howze, who rated the chaplain excellent or superior in nine of the ten categories provided on the form, receiving his lowest mark for "Judgment and Common Sense." In 1951, Kraka was awarded a Bronze Star for his actions near the village of Kunuri, Korea, when the convoy in which he was traveling came under fire while attempting to break through an enemy roadblock. The medal citation reads in part: "With complete disregard for his own safety he moved from one vehicle to another, through heavy enemy fire, administering to and comforting the wounded. Father Kraka's conduct under fire was a source of tremendous inspiration to all who witnessed it and was a major factor in the ultimate success of the convoy in penetrating the roadblock."

In 1957, Major Kraka left the Army to serve as Pastor at

St. John the Baptist Church in the single-traffic-light town of Dover, Indiana. While at St. John's, he personally excavated a 22-foot-deep lake to provide water to the parish buildings, carved a baseball field from the nearby woods, and lobbied successfully to lower Dover's speed limit to 25 miles per hour. Kraka died in 1974 at the age of 67, and is buried in the Priests Circle of Calvary Cemetery in Terre Haute.

The body of **JOHN ELKBERT SHIELDS** was recovered in 1948 after a Melines farmer noticed a "glint in the sun" reflecting from his helmet. The first casualty in the Hotton action was still clutching the grenade he was preparing to throw at the instant he was killed. Shields' parents later donated their son's personal military effects to a Belgian museum, including the bloodstained wallet and cigarette case that he carried in the front breast pockets of his field jacket. John Shields is buried in his hometown cemetery in Ripley, New York.

JACK WARDEN was wounded on March 25, 1945, and never returned to action. Following his discharge, he returned to Texas and worked as a manager for the Wesson Oil Company before starting up a food distribution business. In 1988, Warden was inspired to revisit the events of December 1944, and subsequently assisted numerous veterans and others, including the author, in unraveling the various accounts of the Hotton battle. He lives in Austin.

CHARLIE BRYSON went back to his old desk at the John Hancock Life Insurance Company in Attleboro, Massachusetts, where he retired in 1983. Shortly before his death in 2006, he learned that the citizens of Belgium had placed a plaque on the south shoulder of the Hotton bridge to honor him and the other Americans who had defended the village.

SAM HOGAN returned to action five days after his escape from Marcouray, his task force refitted with new tanks and equipment, and participated in every CCR engagement during the remainder of the war. In 1946, he was appointed to the Allied War Crimes Commission sitting in Ludwigsburg, Germany, prosecuting enemy soldiers charged with killing captured American bomber crews. In 1950, Colonel Hogan earned a law degree from Columbia University, subsequently serving as Judge Adjutant General for the 2nd and 4th Armored Divisions, and with the Defense Intelligence Agency. In 1968, he retired to South America with his wife, where he spent the next 23 years guiding sportsmen through the Ecuadorian jungle. Hogan died in Texas in 2005.

MELVIN BIDDLE was wounded on January 3, 1945, and did not return to action. In September 1945, Biddle was awarded the Medal of Honor for his actions at *Quatre Bras*, credited with killing 17 Germans with 19 shots from his M-1 rifle, and knocking out, unassisted, three enemy machine gun emplacements. President Truman remarked to Biddle during the ceremony on the White House lawn: "People don't believe me when I say I'd rather have this medal than be President." Biddle's heroics led to a career at the Veterans Administration, from which he retired in 1990. His death on December 16,

2010 – the 66th anniversary of the beginning of the Battle of the Bulge – was reported in newspapers across America.

DON FRASER came home after his year of combat without a scratch, and returned to the Blue Island Post Office outside of Chicago where he served as its Postmaster for 30 years. In 1994, he returned to *Quatre Bras* with Bill Boyle and his surviving brothers from the 517th for the dedication of a monument erected in their honor. On that occasion, *Quatre Bras* was rechristened the "517th Carrefour." He died in Florida in 2008.

BILL BOYLE's First Battalion received a Presidential Unit Citation for its "repeated displays of individual and collective gallantry" while attached to Bobby Howze's CCR in Soy. Boyle was awarded the Distinguished Service Cross, America's second highest combat honor, for his extraordinary heroism on *La Roumière*. On January 5, 1945, Boyle was sprayed by a 9-mm machine pistol near Bergeval, Belgium, and spent 21 months undergoing numerous surgeries to regain the use of his arms. Determined to return to duty as an Airborne commander, he declined a full disability and ultimately recovered to lead a combat battalion in Korea. In 1967, then the father of ten children, he retired from the Army to begin a second career as an accountant and tax advisor. Colonel Boyle died in upstate New York in 2009.

DAVE CLAGETT spent nine months recovering from his wounds, married a beautiful nurse and returned to duty. In

1949, he authored a monograph analyzing the operations of the 3rd Battalion, 290th Infantry, at *La Roumière*, including "those factors which contributed most to the excessive expenditure of human lives." At the top of his list was the decision by "higher headquarters" to commit an untried combat unit against an experienced enemy holding a strong defensive position. Clagett went on to serve in various duty stations, including Vietnam, and retired as a Colonel in 1969 following an assignment as Professor of Military Science at the University of Pittsburgh. He died in 1995 and is interred in the Old West Point Chapel Columbarium.

Acknowledgements

THIS BOOK WAS MADE POSSIBLE BY THE SCORES OF VETERANS who graciously returned with me to a place and time they would have preferred to forget. Among them, in memory, are John Anderson, Bill McIntosh, Dewitt Poole, Bob Russell, Sam Pasquali, Al Camurati, George McCain, Bill Rodman, Glenn Shaunce, Bill "Doc" Cohen, Charlie Bryson, Clark Archer, Melvin Biddle, Don Fraser and Bill Boyle. I am also indebted to the families of these forgotten soldiers, particularly the daughters of Robert "Bobby" Howze. Without them there would be no story to tell.

In addition, I thank Luc Vanden Berghe, who enabled me to retrace the routes of Task Force Hogan, the 517th and the 290th; his wife Mia, for her constant cheer and incomparable Belgian soup at the end of those cold days; Lucien Leruth, for opening his museum and allowing me to hold the personal effects of John Shields; Dave Clagett, Jr., who brought his father to life by way of a video interview and other records in which he discussed "that unfortunate affair" on *La Roumière*; Rik Peirson and Annette Jones Howlette, who introduced me to Lieutenants John Peirson and Kenneth Jones, both killed on the hill; and Gil Nelson, Bruce Galbraith and Jake Weisinger, who survived the hill and described what it was like to have been there.

I owe special thanks to Dieter Laes, a young historian whose vast knowledge of *La Bataille des Ardennes*, including the battle for Hotton, enriched my understanding of the events of that dark December in 1944. His manifold contributions rise to the rank of collaboration in the truest sense of the word.

Finally, my thanks to Don Marsh for his astute military perspective and insistence on precision; to Anna Macedo, for her fine copyediting; and to Emily McKeage, for doing what the best editors do for far less than they're worth.

More information and photographs relating
to the Hotton battle can be found at
http://www.finbarpress.com/thehottonreport.html